EMPOWER YOUR FAITH

*Practical Strategies for Women to Prioritize God,
Improve Self-Esteem, and Discover God's Plan for Your Life*

KASHANA RUTH

Scripture Use Acknowledgment
Scripture quotations are taken from the following translations and are identified in-text by their abbreviations (NLT, NIV, KJV, AMP, ESV). All rights reserved by their respective copyright holders. Scripture accessed via YouVersion (www.bible.com).

ISBN: 979-8-9924985-0-9 - Paperback
eISBN: 979-8-9924985-1-6 - eBook

Printed in the United States of America

Cover Design: Sherilyn Bennett of Camden Lane Creative

Photo: Prentice Ruth

Editors: Joel Boyce of JCB Educational Services and Hmd Publishing

For more information, please visit:

www.womencultivatedinchrist.com

www.eyfbook.com

DEDICATIONS

To the women who have shaped me—my biological mother, mother-in-love, and stepmom; my sisters, aunties, cousins, and my only living grandmother; my lifelong friends who became sisters; every woman God has placed in my life to love me, challenge me, cover me in prayer, or call me higher; and to my daughter—when you're old enough to understand, may this book be a launching pad into your own bold, Spirit-led journey—this is for you.

To the real you, the one behind the perfectly posed selfies and color-coded planners. The one who shows up for everyone else but quietly wonders who's showing up for her. The one who keeps it all together in public, but battles silent battles in private. The multitasker, the overachiever, the prayer warrior in progress. The one tired of pretending and finally ready to be seen by God, and led by Him.

This is for the woman who's done being driven by pressure and is finally ready to be led by purpose. You've felt the tug. That holy discontent. The knowing that there's more, *and guess what?* There *is so much* more, and it's already tucked inside of you by the One who created you. This book is your permission slip to grow, heal, and show up fully as the woman God designed—flaws, faith, and all. He sees the masterpiece, even when you feel like a hot mess in a messy bun.

So here's to bold faith, fresh vision, and confidence that can't be shaken, because it's anchored in Him. Let this be the season you stop striving and start surrendering. May God restore your confidence, renew your vision, and reroute your steps straight into His divine plan. Let's be honest. Success without God is just spiritual exhaustion in cute heels or tennis shoes.

You were made for more; this is your *official* invitation to walk in it.

LIVING LEGACY:
A WORD FROM MY GRANNY, ELINOR PHILLIPS

As I reflect on my journey of faith, purpose, and obedience, I am reminded of the legacy I come from. My granny, Elinor Phillips, is a woman of quiet strength and timeless wisdom. She had ten children, five beautiful girls and five handsome boys, and built a life grounded in love, faith, and family.

When I asked her if she had anything she wanted to share with the women reading this book, she reminded me of something powerful.

Granny often talks about her late husband, my grandfather, who was an excellent provider and leader for their home. She never fails to express how well he loved her and was committed to caring for his family.

Through her words, she encouraged me, and now encourages you, to carry that same spirit forward. Be a woman who honors God in how you serve, lead, and provide for your home. Love your family well. Treat your husband with respect and build your household with wisdom and grace. Above all else, trust that everything else will fall into place when God is first.

This is the kind of living legacy she's passed down to me. At 85 years young, she still speaks with the same clarity and love that shaped our family. Now, I pass it down to you.

— *With love always,*

Kashana Ruth, on behalf of Elinor Phillips

CONTENTS

INTRODUCTION

A Love Letter to the Woman Who's Ready for More

To the Cultivated Woman who knows there's more to life than what meets the eye, welcome. Whether you're curled up on the couch with your favorite throw blanket, squeezed into a five-minute break at work, or hiding out in your car for peace, this moment is divine timing.

Welcome to *Empower Your Faith: Practical Strategies for Women to Prioritize God, Improve Self-Esteem, and Discover God's Plan for* Your Life, and thank you for purchasing this book. My hope is that by the time you reach the end of this book, you will have the resources and knowledge to develop a deeper relationship with God, enhance clarity on where your life is headed, and gain confidence to walk in authority according to whom God has called you to be.

If you are reading this book, then I know you have a desire to develop a deeper relationship with God and seek His will for your life. However, you have been struggling to make time for God due to busy schedules, work-life balance issues, distractions, and a lack of self-discipline or low self-esteem.

You may have been seeking God for answers, but have difficulty being consistent and fully submitting your life to Him. You may be wondering if He hears your prayers or why He seems distant from you. I can relate because this was my experience for several years before recommitting my life to Christ. You spend your life prioritizing your career or job, personal life, social life, etc, while God is left with the residuals of whatever you have left over from the day, if any.

You may feel like your identity is in your career, job title, personal titles, or anything of worldly satisfaction. You may find yourself relying on self-will by doing the things you think are necessary to live a meaningful life. Maybe you're unsure how to develop a deeper relationship with God. You may find yourself thinking: *How should I pray? How do I fully submit to God? When or how should I fast?*

I wrote this book to remind you that you can have an intimate relationship with God while juggling your careers, jobs, and personal life. You don't have to be a pastor, bishop, apostle, or any other ministry leader to hear from God. It can still happen even if you feel like you've wasted years of your life. God's faithfulness never ends, and His mercies are always new. This means that no matter how far off-track you feel, it's never too late to return to God.

I was this same woman a few years ago. During my journey, I have overcome being distracted and gained self-discipline. I have overcome finding my identity through worldly views by finding my identity through Christ. I have overcome relying on my own will by totally submitting to God's will. I have overcome a lack of prayer life, a lack of fasting, and a lack of studying the Word, and I have turned these all into a lifestyle. Over the past couple of years, I have had the pleasure to advise and mentor others with the same struggles as me, but it wasn't always this way.

I remember there was a point in my life when I didn't have an intimate relationship with God. I depended on my academic achievements to satisfy me, hoping to fill the void of something missing in my life. It's like each degree that I finished, I desired more. I remember completing my bachelor's degree, and I still had this feeling of incompleteness. Then, I went on to get my master's degree because I thought that maybe I was working too hard, and I felt that a master's degree would help slow things down, because I would be in a position with more autonomy. However, when I finished, I still had the same old feeling that something was missing. Then, I went on to think that maybe it was because I hadn't found the right job, but each time, I realized that assumption wasn't the answer. How could this be? I had a wonderful family, a nice home, and a great career, but I still felt like I was lacking.

I sought God to discover why I had those feelings, and He eventually revealed to me that the missing component was Him. Once I realized this, I began to spend more time in prayer, but it wasn't always consistent. I'd be on fire for a few weeks, waking up early, praying like a warrior, and then boom! Spiritual snooze button activated. I was a part-time prayer warrior with full-time distractions, and if spiritual inconsistency had a loyalty program, I had platinum status. I would only read the verse of the day in my Bible app, but I never went any further than that. I would rather sleep in or go to bed at a decent time instead of getting my prayer and study time in. I prioritized my family and work life first. It wouldn't get done if I didn't have time or the energy after family and work things were handled.

This was a continuous cycle for years of doing the bare minimum and being a lackadaisical Christian. It was like being on a spiritual treadmill, with lots of motion and little progress. I was running, but still in the same place with God. I was not growing efficiently in my walk with Christ. I felt stuck and unsure of how not only to make the time but also to be consistent. How in the world was I going to break this? My desire was never fully met until one day, I was listening to a sermon that spoke about laying down our lives for God's life, fully submitting to Him, and desiring His will for our lives. I was convicted. It became clear to me that I was living by my own will and not by God's will. I was fed up with my excuses, so I decided from that point on that I would fully recommit my life to Christ and be intentional in growing closer to Him and studying His word. The years I spent feeling like I was lacking something finally made a turnaround, and I had joy and total fulfillment in my life. It was like I'd discovered the VIP access to peace, and guess what? God had been holding the door open the whole time.

Recommitting my life to Christ has changed my life. I have developed an intimate relationship with God by staying committed to prayer and studying His word. I have developed self-discipline and learned how to put God first while juggling my career and personal life. I am better able to discern His voice when He is speaking. I have increased my self-confidence because I know who I am through Christ. Eventually, after being consistent for some time, God began to reveal one of the callings upon my life: writing this book. None of this would have been possible had I not recommitted my life to Christ and allowed Him to take the lead.

As I began walking closer with God, He revealed a transformational process to me, a spiritual and practical alignment strategy, and I would like to share it with you. I call it the Cultivated BOSS Method™: Bold in Faith, Obedient to God's Call, Spirit-led and Surrendered, and Strategic for Kingdom Impact. This method helped me not only break free from surface-level faith but also gave me a blueprint to live boldly and purposefully, aligned with Heaven's agenda. The Cultivated Woman is a BOSS, Bold in faith, Obedient to God's voice, Spirit-led and surrendered in her daily decisions, and Strategic in how she advances Kingdom impact.

The purpose of Empower Your Faith: Practical Strategies for Women to Prioritize God, Improve Self-esteem, and Discover God's Plan for Your Life is to help guide and equip you through your journey of placing God at the center of your life, so you can refocus your values and visions, increase your self-esteem, and dominate the path God has for you.

However, here's something I want you to know from the start—this book isn't just about strategies; it's about real stories, transformation, and seeing yourself in the bigger picture of God's plan. So grab your journal, favorite pen, and maybe even a treat (*yes, even the snack that makes you feel slightly guilty*), because we're diving deep. This isn't your average Bible study; it's time to get *Bold, Obedient, Spirit-Led,* and *Strategic*! Throughout each chapter, I'll be sharing parts of my personal journey, not the polished version, but the honest one. I'll take you behind the scenes of my struggles, doubts, and breakthroughs. Alongside that, I'll be introducing you to powerful women from the Bible who walked through hardship, heartache, and moments of bold faith.

You'll read about women like Esther, Ruth, Deborah, and many more, and I want you to see yourself in them. As you read their stories, I challenge you to ask: *How do their journeys mirror mine? What can I learn from their faith?* My prayer is that through their stories and mine, you'll find encouragement, empowerment, and evidence that God can use *your* life, just as He used theirs.

Don't just read this book—experience it. Let each chapter stir something within you. Picture yourself walking in their sandals. Imagine how their obedience, courage, and surrender brought about breakthroughs, and then believe that God can do the same through you.

I encourage every reader of this book to embrace the strategies learned. Each chapter will have strategies to implement into your daily life. To reap the benefits from this book, I highly recommend you pray before each time you read the book and invite the Holy Spirit to give you a deeper understanding of who He is and provide spiritual insight into your life. I also encourage you to keep a journal handy to reflect on what God is saying to you and take action on the strategies mentioned.

Do not delay your relationship with God any further. You cannot be fully fulfilled until you fully submit to God. Once you read *Empower Your Faith: Practical Strategies for Women to Prioritize God, Improve Self-esteem, and Discover God's Plan for Your Life*, you will be equipped to grow deeper with God, discover your calling, and impact the world. Don't just skim through this book like another self-help read. I'm inviting you into a transformation. To turn off the spiritual snooze button, silence the inner critic, and say YES to walking hand-in-hand with your Creator, daily, boldly, and without apology. Tomorrow is not promised, and lukewarm living won't cut it. Let's stop giving God the leftovers and start giving Him the main dish because success means nothing if God isn't in it, and BOSS woman, you were made for more than microwave faith. So rise up, adjust your crown, and walk like the daughter of the King you are.

With Love,

Kashana

OPENING DECLARATION

I Am Becoming a Cultivated BOSS Affirmation

Declare this over yourself:

I am becoming a Cultivated BOSS. A Cultivated BOSS is a woman who is Bold, Obedient, Spirit-Led, and Strategic for Kingdom Impact. I may not have it all figured out yet, but I choose to walk by faith. I am open to God's voice, ready to obey, and willing to grow. This journey is not just about information. It's about transformation. I believe God is calling me higher, and I am here for it.

Heart Prep Prayer: Speak, Believe, Receive

Pray this out loud:

Lord, I invite You into this journey. Prepare my heart, renew my mind, and open my spirit to what You want to reveal. Help me not just to learn, but to be transformed. Align my desires with Your will, and give me the courage to walk boldly in obedience. Let every word I read draw me closer to You. In Jesus' name, Amen.

CHAPTER 1
KNOW YOUR CREATOR

> *"The key to understanding life is in the source of life,*
> *not in life itself"*
> **(Munroe, 2021, p. 220).**

When "Success" Still Feels Empty

Have you ever felt that "something was missing" in your life but couldn't quite put your finger on it? I know I have. I sought out superficial things I thought were the answer to the problem, only to discover that the feeling was still there. The answer didn't become clear until I realized I had achieved everything I wanted in life, but I lacked a true relationship with God. I put so much time into being a wife and mom, earning my degrees, and landing the perfect job while treating God like an old acquaintance. *You know, the kind you only text when you need something?* Yep. That kind of old acquaintance. We're taught that success means staying busy, but busyness without purpose leads to burnout, and burnout is often a sign we're building without the builder.

> 🗨**Real Talk Moment:**
> Success without God at the center is a fancy version of being lost. Don't confuse a packed schedule with a *fulfilled* soul.

I didn't realize that my relationship with God was lacking until about five years ago when I started my journey working towards anesthesia school. I was working as a brand-new nurse practitioner. I was the main provider in charge at a nursing home during the mornings, and in the afternoons, I would go over to a psychiatric hospital to help manage the patients medically. Despite all my accomplishments, I felt restless, as if I was still searching for something greater, something beyond myself.

Esther's Wake-Up Call and Mine

This feeling of longing reminds me of Queen Esther's journey. She was an orphan, a young Jewish girl with no idea that she was destined for something greater. When she was chosen as queen, she could have easily settled into her position, enjoying the comforts of the palace and being content with the life she had unexpectedly received. However, God had placed her there for more than just comfort—He positioned her for a Divine assignment. When her people faced annihilation, she was called to step forward, putting her own life at risk. She had a cousin named Mordecai who also became her guardian after her parents died. Esther could have remained silent, living in the palace, keeping to herself, but Mordecai's words to her were profound. He told her, "Who knows if perhaps you were made queen for just such a time as this?" (Esther 4:14, NLT). That moment became her defining shift. She recognized that her position wasn't about her own comfort but fulfilling a God-ordained purpose.

Like Esther and many other women, I was in a place of comfort and security, or at least that's what I thought, but deep inside, there was an unsettling feeling, a whisper in my spirit that told me there was more. I was so focused on the next career move that I didn't realize God had placed me in a transition season, not to move forward in my own plans but to step into His purpose. Just as Esther had to make a choice to trust God and walk in obedience, I had to make a decision. Esther had to shift her mindset from comfort to calling. *What area of your life feels comfortable but may be keeping you from your greater purpose?* That was the question I didn't even realize I was wrestling with. Would I continue chasing my plans, or would I surrender and trust the path He was revealing? Spoiler alert: God's plan didn't come with a 5-step checklist or Pinterest board, but it did come with peace and a whole lot of refining. Not All Doors Are Destinations

I wasn't happy with my first nurse practitioner position for multiple reasons—a lack of training, constant changes in the facilities I covered, and the uncertainty of being new to the role. After about two months, I started praying about my next step, specifically, I wanted God to tell me if enrolling in anesthesia school was the right move. I told God, "If this is for me, open the door. If not, show me another way." I got an unexpected meeting request from my boss a couple of weeks later. Immediately, my mind went to I wonder what the meeting was about. *Could this be about my performance?* The day of the meeting came, and as I sat in the conference room anxiously waiting, my boss informed me that my position would soon be phased out because the nursing home was hiring an in-house company to take over. Then, he offered to open another position for me, but as soon as I heard the words 'phasing out,' I felt relief wash over me. This was my ticket out. My mind was racing with thoughts. *This is it! This is my way out!*

It's funny now that I am thinking back on it. My boss and manager looked as if they were breaking bad news to me, but inside, I was rejoicing. They were breaking the news like I had just been fired from my dream job. Meanwhile, I was sitting there like, 'Cue the praise break music!' God had answered my prayers. After he finished talking, they sat and waited for my response about whether I would accept the new position. I said, "No, that's okay. I'm fine with the position phasing out." Their looks went from sympathy to confusion. The Lord knows I wanted to be transparent and tell them I didn't like the job, that they needed to improve a few things, and that God had heard my prayers, but I contained myself. This was my way out, and it had come so unexpectedly. They accepted that I declined the new role and I agreed to finish out my last month there. *Think back to a door that closed in your life. It may have felt like rejection at the time, but looking back, was God protecting or redirecting you?*

A Divine Exit Before the Storm

What I didn't know at the time was that God was orchestrating something far greater. A week after my meeting, I received even bigger news. The facility I had worked in was about to be converted into a COVID-19 facility. This was the start of the COVID-19 pandemic, so no one really knew what was going on. We just knew there was a virus causing a bunch of people to get sick, and the death toll was on the rise. They told me that I had less than a week to clear all of my patients out and have them transferred to another nursing home facility. Both facilities where I worked went on lockdown. Masks were mandatory. Residents and staff were panicked because we didn't know what we were up against. Half of the world went on lockdown. We weren't allowed out of our homes unless it was mandatory or if we needed essentials. I remember when I would leave for work during that time, I had to carry a printed document saying I was a healthcare provider. Nothing says *apocalypse vibes* like flashing a badge just to have permission to be out on the streets. This was definitely a scary time for us all!

I had never experienced anything like that in my life before. It was a period of crisis, and saying this was a very stressful time for me is an understatement. After a few days, I had all of my patients transferred to different nursing home facilities where they were assigned, along with their required updated medical charts. I had unknowingly been pulled out of my job just before one of the most chaotic and overwhelming times in healthcare history.

God saw me through it, and my husband and I couldn't believe how fast everything transpired. We were fortunate enough that my husband had a great job, and I was able to be off work from March to December. The timeline worked out perfectly because eventually, all of the schools went on lockdown due to the virus, and our daughter was in 1st grade at the time. We needed someone to be home to help with her e-learning. Our son didn't have eLearning because he was in an early learning program, but I had to be home, caring for him and teaching him as well. *You see how God moves?* I can't imagine how hard it would've been with my husband and me both working with all of this going on. Back then, I saw it as God simply opening a door for me to go back to school, but now I realize He was doing so much more. He was working things out for me behind the scenes, sheltering me from a storm that was about to hit. He pulled me out of the workplace just before the COVID-19 pandemic struck hard. Looking back, I see that God was trying to get me to be still—to step away from the chaos and draw closer to Him. This was His way of redirecting and positioning me for what was to come.

Maybe you've experienced something similar. A door closed unexpectedly, and it didn't make sense at the time. However, when you look back, you realize it was God's protection. *Have you ever had a situation like that? Have you had a moment when you later saw how God was moving behind the scenes, or have you had a time when what you thought was a detour was a Divine setup?*

Ignoring the Red Flags

Here's the truth—I should never have taken that job in the first place. When I first applied, I had this uneasy feeling, but I ignored it. *Why?* I was desperate. After graduating with my master's degree, I spent months searching for my first nurse practitioner job while still working the floor as an RN. When the opportunity came, I jumped on it, even though I knew something wasn't right deep down. That's a lesson in itself. Sometimes, we rush ahead of God because we don't want to wait. We act like patience is optional until God makes waiting our only assignment. We settle for something we weren't meant to have because we think it's our only option. The truth is, God always has something better. That experience taught me that desperation can cloud discernment, but God, in His mercy, will often redirect us even when we ignore His first nudges. Desperation makes detours look like destiny, but peace is often the signpost that tells you you're on the right path.

> **🗨Real Talk Moment**:
> God will never rush you into anything that requires you to lose your peace. If it costs you clarity, it's too expensive.

When I think about it, I see how God had been positioning me just like He had positioned Esther. At the time, it didn't make complete sense, but God was setting the stage for something I didn't expect. He wasn't just redirecting my career path; He was setting me apart for something bigger, calling me to draw closer to Him and truly seek His purpose for my life.

Esther had a moment of realization when she understood that she had been placed in the palace, not for herself. She was placed there to be an instrument of deliverance for her people. In the same way, it took me years to realize that my career was never just about my personal ambitions—it was about positioning myself to be an instrument for God's will. Although it took me a while to grasp this, God was patient and continued to lead me until I saw the bigger picture.

When You Chase the Dream Before the Confirmation

After praying and seeking confirmation, I came to truly believe that God was leading me to pursue a career in anesthesia school. I felt a strong pull toward the field of nurse anesthesia, one that excited me and inspired me to dream big. I envisioned myself becoming a certified registered nurse anesthetist (CRNA), holding a doctoral degree, managing patients with confidence, and eventually opening my own business.

CRNAs are advanced practice nurses who specialize in anesthesia, the powerful medication used to prevent pain during surgeries and procedures. They care for patients before, during, and after anesthesia is given. I was excited to learn how to intubate, place central lines, and improve my critical thinking skills under pressure. I loved the idea of working with one patient at a time and having more autonomy. I could see it all so clearly, but here's the thing: I never truly received confirmation before making this huge decision.

Looking back, I assumed God would approve it simply because my intentions were good. I believed that if I worked hard and meant well, He'd surely approve the plan, but in all actuality, I jumped ahead. I didn't pause long enough to ask and wait for clarity. I started the journey first, then asked Him to bless it second. Some nights, I would have dreams of talking with the CRNA program director or rounding on patients as a CRNA, but sometimes I would wonder if those were divine revelations or just the desires of my heart playing out in my sleep.

What was one of the first major roadblocks? I needed at least one year of critical care experience to apply for the program, but my nurse practitioner degree focused on family care, not critical care. ICU positions were rarely open to NPs like me, *so guess what I had to do?* I had to take a step back. I returned to work as a registered nurse in the intensive care unit, and let me tell you, when I made that decision, folks looked at me like I had lost my mind. Like, *"You're leaving your cushy NP job to go where?"* but what they didn't understand was the assignment. This was something I hadn't done before, and I wasn't exactly eager to do it. It wasn't a demotion, but it definitely felt like a detour. Since I could only work part-time, it took me two full years to complete that requirement, and that was just the beginning. CRNA school has some of the toughest admission requirements I've ever seen. Just to apply, I had to:

- Write a 500-word personal statement
- Submit three letters of recommendation
- Shadow multiple CRNAs (I completed four shadowing sessions)
- Pass the CCRN certification exam, which took months of studying
- Complete a graduate-level statistics course in just six weeks
- Finally, an interview with the admissions committee through both a written and oral exam on critical care topics

I even joined two professional organizations designed specifically to support aspiring CRNAs. Looking back, I still can't believe how much I pushed myself. I was laser-focused, determined, and motivated, but I was also striving more than surrendering. Here's the truth I didn't fully realize at the time. I was including God *partially* when He should've been leading me *completely. Have you ever done that? Have you ever pursued something good, maybe even something you thought God was on board with, but you leaned more on your own effort than His strength?* My desire for success wasn't wrong, but somewhere along the way, my focus shifted. I became more consumed with the goal than with God. I started relying on my grind instead of His grace, and that's a dangerous place to be.

When Favor Meets Faith: The Job, The Waitlist, and the Butterflies

After completing all the intense requirements for CRNA school and gaining the critical care experience I needed, the moment I had worked so hard for finally arrived. It was time to apply.

I submitted my application and later found out I did not get accepted into school. During this time, I left my role as an ICU nurse to return to my nurse practitioner roots—this time, at a pain clinic. Let me tell you that this was by far the best job I had ever had. I was the main provider when the owner wasn't there. The role was clear, the schedule was flexible, and the training was top-tier. I felt supported and confident, and settled for the first time in a long time. K-LOVE played softly in the background every day, filling the clinic with Christian music and peace. The staff was kind. The atmosphere was uplifting. I could even pray with patients and share the gospel when I felt led to do so. It was more than just a job. It felt like a *Godsend,* and it was.

Before applying, I had prayed over the position. It felt aligned—both professionally and spiritually. The role was still tied into anesthesia through chronic pain management, and more importantly, I sensed God's hand all over it. Then came the first confirmation. During my initial phone interview, I was on the road with one of my sisters, and suddenly, I started seeing monarch butterflies over and over again. Monarch butterflies are symbolic of spiritual transformation and rebirth. I couldn't help but feel like God was speaking through the details. I did well in that interview and was invited for a second in-person interview. Before going, I asked God for another confirmation. I prayed, "Lord, if this job is truly for me, let everything go smoothly and let the pay be negotiable."

Guess what? Not only was the pay negotiable, but I received the maximum offer. Even better, the owner personally adjusted my schedule, so I could get my kids off to school in the mornings *and* be home before my husband left for work in the evenings. No compromising. No convincing. Just grace and Divine alignment.

Then came the *third* confirmation. On the way to that in-person interview, I saw another swarm of monarch butterflies. This time, they danced across the sky for nearly a mile. I was on the phone with one of my best friends. I stared in amazement and said, "I don't know what's going on in this town, but there are butterflies everywhere." When I arrived for the interview, I even asked the office manager, "Do you all usually have this many butterflies out here?" She laughed and said, "No… we just have cornfields. I don't remember the last time I saw butterflies like that." At that point, I knew God was with me. But let me pause and say this: confirmation from God won't always come with butterflies floating across your windshield. Sometimes, it's a deep, unshakable peace in your spirit, even when things don't make sense on paper. Other times, the opposite is an unsettling feeling in your gut that won't go away, no matter how perfect the opportunity looks. *That uneasiness?* That's a form of confirmation, too.

This is why we must be spiritually in tune. God doesn't just speak through signs and wonders; He often speaks through conviction, peace, discomfort, or a word whispered in the quiet place. Sometimes, it'll be through wise counsel, repeated Scriptures, or even a personal sign that only you and God understand. The key isn't to look for signs everywhere, it's to stay close enough to Him that when He does speak, you don't miss it.

The interview went smoothly. I was offered the job and thrived in that role for almost two years. Then came the shift. It was time to apply for anesthesia school again. I applied for a second time and was placed on the waiting list. It was not a rejection, but it was not an acceptance either. Still, I felt an unusual peace. The program was highly competitive, accepting only a limited number of students once per year, and students weren't allowed to work while they were enrolled. That's when the owner and I had a conversation. He needed someone who could be committed long-term, and I couldn't make that promise. We agreed it was time for me to transition out. Even without a guaranteed spot in the program, I felt led to let it go.

The clinic owner even offered me a partnership opportunity to stay and build something long-term with him. On paper, it was a dream offer. Everything about it seemed ideal—the flexibility, the income, the influence. However, deep down, something didn't sit right. Every time I seriously considered staying, I felt a strong check in my spirit—a quiet, unwavering whisper that said, "If you stay, you'll regret it." It almost felt like a distraction—like the enemy was dangling comfort and security in front of me to pull me off course. It was subtle and tempting, but I knew better. Sometimes, the most dangerous detours come dressed as good opportunities.

Have you ever felt a tension between your comfort and your calling? Your heart craves stability, but has your spirit ever felt that there's more? I couldn't shake it, so I made the decision to walk away and trust God. I decided to believe that the peace I felt in prayer wasn't lying to me. As my last days at the clinic approached, I kept praying: *Lord, am I really going to get into school? Should I look for another job in the meantime?* These questions alone reflected moments of doubt. What I should've been doing was declaring that it was already done.

Each time, I felt peace. I felt as if God was saying, *Don't worry. I've got this.* I didn't search. I waited. I decided to leave my cushy nurse practitioner position *again*, and yes, people were looking at me *once again* like, *"What are you doing? We've already been through this once!"* I even remember one of my coworkers shaking her head and saying, *"Honey, you're out here looking for a pot of gold when it's right in front of you."* We both laughed, but everyone's comments started making me second-guess everything. Was I doing too much? Was I missing what was right in front of me? Still, deep down, I knew I had to stay the course and go where I felt led.

Then... nothing. No call. No acceptance. I didn't get off the waitlist. I was stunned. No job. No program. Just silence. I stared at my inbox like it owed me an apology, and I was ready to file a Holy Ghost complaint form. I sat with God and asked: *Why? Why give me peace if the outcome was going to be disappointment? Why did it all feel so right, only to leave me here, stuck in the in-between?* I didn't get immediate answers, but I *did* get a deeper resolve. Four months later, I applied again. This was my third time.

I was invited for another interview, but everything had changed. The questions differed completely from previous rounds, and I was caught off guard. If you could've been a fly on the wall, I looked like a deer in headlights and not a cute cartoon Bambi kind, more like *Jesus, take the whole steering wheel* energy.

I walked out feeling crushed. I thought I had bombed the first half of the interview, even though I did well during the second. There was nothing left to do. I had prepared. I had prayed. Now, it was up to God.

Esther also faced uncertainty when she prepared to approach the king uninvited. She knew that stepping forward could mean death, but she fasted, sought God, and took the step of faith anyway. Her obedience led to the deliverance of her people. She didn't know the outcome when she first stepped forward, but trusted God to guide her.

That was my lesson—trusting God in uncertainty. Even when things didn't go the way I expected, I had to believe that He was leading me to something greater. It wasn't about my own timing; it was about being positioned for His purpose.

Surrendering My Plans: Choosing God's Will Over My Own

Are you inviting God into the journey... or asking Him to bless what you've already decided? Be honest. He can handle it. I remember one quiet evening, just a few weeks after my third school interview, sitting in my prayer closet. The closet was dim, peaceful, and sacred. I had come to read a few written prayers, but before I could finish, I felt the Holy Spirit prompting me to shift. He said, *Move into worship*, so I lifted my voice, and as I began to worship, I heard His gentle whisper in my spirit: *Press in more. Praise Him more.* I did as He commanded. I poured out my heart in worship, lifting His name higher with every word. Something deep within me broke like a wall crashing down. Tears began to fall. I wasn't just worshipping anymore. I was *declaring*. Declaring who He is. Declaring His goodness. Surrendering everything. In the middle of that moment, a deep conviction washed over me: *I don't care what I want anymore—I only care about what You want, Lord.* I sobbed like a baby, not out of sadness, but because His presence was so overwhelming, so near, and so real.

> **🗨Real Talk Moment:**
> Sometimes the breakdown is the breakthrough. Don't fight the tears, they're evidence that you're finally letting God in.

Through the tears, I whispered, *"God, if anesthesia school isn't Your will for me, I don't want it. I just want You. Whatever You want me to do, that's what I'll do because with You by my side, I can't fail."* Let me tell you, it takes the Holy Spirit's power to walk away from something you once prayed for, as if it were the answer to *everything.* In that still moment, I sensed His response deep in my spirit. He said, *Finally... you see. Finally... you understand.* It was as if heaven smiled. Looking back, I realize something important. I used to pray, *"Lord, I want to get into anesthesia school... if it's Your will..."* However, honestly and deep down, I didn't really mean the "if" part of my statement. I wanted what I wanted. I had already made up my mind, and I just wanted His stamp of approval.

Have you ever done that? Have you ever prayed for God's will, but secretly, you hoped it matched your own plans? I didn't realize it then, but I had idolized anesthesia school. It had become the thing I thought about constantly. The thing I chased. The thing I was willing to sacrifice everything for—even intimacy with God. Here's what I learned. You know something has become an idol when it consumes your thoughts, shapes your decisions, and takes priority over your time with God. When your joy, identity, or peace depends more on that thing than on Him, it's no longer just a dream—it's a distraction. That night in the prayer closet changed everything. It was the first time I fully surrendered. It was the first time I laid down what I thought mattered most to pick up what *God* said mattered most. That's what it means to truly know Him.

To say, "Even if it costs me my dream, I choose You," *means that you are connected to Him,* because when you really know your Creator, you realize that choosing Him is choosing life. Finding Him is finding *yourself.* I had spent years pouring into the dream of anesthesia school, but I thank God for showing me what it truly means to walk in His will. Looking back, I can see it clearly now.

God was calling me *out* of my nurse practitioner position, not for the preparation for anesthesia school to be a distraction, but to pull me *closer* to Him. However, at the time, I didn't see it. I was so focused on checking the next box, chasing the next title, and climbing the ladder of success. Now, don't get me wrong, there's nothing wrong with climbing the ladder of success. The problem comes when we don't place God at the center of our plans, and truthfully, my heart was in the wrong place.

I let my desire for anesthesia school take the lead.

It wasn't that the dream itself was bad, but it had become a hidden checkbox rooted in my own ambition. A quiet voice within me was whispering, *If I just achieve this, I'll finally feel fulfilled.* I was striving, and slowly, without realizing it, I was drifting.

The truth? I missed it for years. I didn't recognize how God was gently trying to re-center my heart. He had to draw me away from the pain clinic, not because it was a bad place, but because of the season He was preparing me for. He needed me to disconnect from the noise of work and selfish ambitions, so I could grow deeper in Him. *Have you ever been so locked in on a goal that you didn't even realize your time with God was shrinking?* A clear sign you're missing the bigger picture is when your quiet time with the Lord gets minimized for the *thing* you're chasing.

An example can be when your devotional life becomes dry, rushed, or nonexistent, not because you stopped loving God but because you started loving your plans more. It's a hard truth, but it is one that brings so much freedom once we realize it. We have to check our posture. Are we postured for ourselves, or are we postured where God wants us to be?

Who's to say anesthesia school isn't still a part of my future? It could be very well, but if I ever step into that door, it has to be because *God* is leading me, not because *I'm* pushing my own way in. Now, I understand that my time at the pain clinic wasn't random; it was purposeful preparation. God was using that season not only to soften my heart and reset my focus but also to help me discover who I truly was in Him. He placed me there to grow spiritually, to be a light in the workplace, and to minister to patients and co-workers who needed His love the most. He was getting me ready for something deeper. As you continue reading this book, I'll share more about how that next season looked and how God began to unfold His real assignment for my life.

Who Is God Really?

Before fully trusting God, you need to know who He is, not just what you've heard, but who He reveals Himself to be. He is not distant or unpredictable. He is deeply personal, and He longs to be known. The more you understand His nature, the more confidence you'll gain in following Him. Here are just a few of the powerful attributes of your Creator:

- **Faithful**- God keeps His promises. He is trustworthy—even when we fall short. *"If we are faithless, He remains faithful, for He cannot deny Himself."* — 2 Timothy 2:13

- **All-Knowing (Omniscient)**- He sees the beginning, the end, and every detail in between. *"I make known the end from the beginning, from ancient times, what is still to come."* — Isaiah 46:10

- **All-Present (Omnipresent)**- You are never alone. God is with you in every season, place, and moment. *"Where can I go from Your Spirit? Where can I flee from Your presence?"* — Psalm 139:7

- **Powerful (Omnipotent)**- He has all power in His hands. No situation is too big for Him to handle. *"For nothing will be impossible with God."* — Luke 1:37

- **Loving**- His love is unconditional. You don't have to earn it—it's who He is. *"But God proves His own love for us in that while we were still sinners, Christ died for us."* — Romans 5:8

- **Holy**- He is set apart, pure, and perfect. He calls us to walk in holiness, too. *"But just as He who called you is holy, so be holy in all you do."* — 1 Peter 1:15

- **Just**- God is fair and righteous. He sees every injustice and will bring truth to light. *"The Lord is known by His justice."* — Psalm 9:16

- **Gracious**- He extends unmerited favor and kindness, even when we don't deserve it. *"But He gives more grace. Therefore, it says, 'God opposes the proud but gives grace to the humble."* — James 4:6

- **Merciful**- God withholds the punishment we deserve and offers compassion instead. *"The Lord is merciful and gracious, slow to anger and abounding in steadfast love."* —Psalm 103:8

- **Unchanging**- In a world that constantly shifts, He remains the same. *"Jesus Christ is the same yesterday and today and forever."* — Hebrews 13:8

- **Your Creator**- He formed you with intention and purpose. You are not a mistake. *"Before I formed you in the womb, I knew you, before you were born I set you apart."* —Jeremiah 1:5

Titles of God That Reveal His Heart

Throughout the Bible, God revealed Himself through different names and titles—each one revealing a specific aspect of who He is:

- **El Shaddai** – God Almighty
- **Jehovah Jireh** – The Lord Will Provide
- **Abba** – Father
- **Jehovah Rapha** – The Lord Who Heals
- **El Roi** – The God Who Sees Me
- **Jehovah Shalom** – The Lord Is Peace
- **The Good Shepherd** – He guides and protects you

These aren't just titles, they are promises. When you begin to understand who God really is, you stop questioning whether He sees you, loves you, or has a plan for you. You start to live from a place of assurance. A place of peace. A place of identity rooted in truth.

> **💬Real Talk Moment:**
> You won't follow a God you don't know. If you want to walk boldly in your calling, it starts by becoming deeply rooted in who He is.

What Does It Actually Mean to Know God?

Knowing God isn't about religion or routine. It's not just checking off devotionals or attending services. It's about intimacy. Not Sunday-morning-only intimacy. I'm talking about the *"tell God everything from your fears to your hair appointment"* kind of intimacy. To know God is to walk with Him daily. It's hearing His voice in quiet moments and choosing His way when your way feels easier. It means inviting Him into every detail of your life and trusting Him enough to surrender your plans to Him when they don't align with His plans. It's learning His heart through Scripture, listening for His guidance in prayer, and being transformed in His presence. It's being able to say, "Even when I don't understand what's happening around me, I trust the One who holds it all together."

> 🗨 **Real Talk Moment:**
> You don't need to have the full picture when you trust the One who painted it. Faith doesn't require sight. It requires surrender.

I realized that just as Esther had to surrender her own comfort and step into her calling, I had to release my grip on my own plans and allow God to lead me. Everything changed when I finally let go of my own desires and fully trusted Him. I saw my journey differently. I saw my purpose differently. God had been trying to get my attention all along, but I was missing it. Like Esther, I had been placed in my circumstances for a reason, but it wasn't about me but fulfilling His greater plan. I was no longer just chasing a career. I was stepping into my Divine assignment.

Lessons from Esther

1. God positions us for a purpose. Even when we don't understand it, He is always working behind the scenes.

2. Faith requires action. Esther had to take the bold step of going before the king. Likewise, we must trust God and walk in obedience.

3. Surrender leads to clarity. When Esther chose to align with God's will, her purpose became clear. The same happens when we fully submit to Him.

4. Timing is everything. Esther waited for the right moment to approach the king, just as we must trust God's perfect timing in our own lives.

Just as Esther stepped into her calling, I now understand that God had been preparing me all along, and if you're feeling lost or uncertain, know that God is positioning you, too. You were created for such a time as this.

Tangible Ways to Deepen Your Connection with God

Here are a few strategies to help you get to know God on a personal level.

1. Recommit to God – If you've drifted, take a moment to realign. Make God your priority again through prayer and godly influences. Say this prayer: *Heavenly Father, I've fallen short. I recommit my life to You. Cleanse me, renew me, and fill me with Your Spirit. Lead me to walk in Your will. In Jesus's name, Amen.*

2. Prioritize Time with God – Set daily moments for prayer, worship, and reflection, starting with 10-15 minutes.

3. Choose an Easy-to-Understand Bible - Read Scripture daily and consider using a study Bible for deeper insight.

4. Find Scriptures for Growth - Write down any negative emotions you're experiencing, look up Bible verses that counter them, and speak these verses daily.

5. Meditate and Memorize Scripture - Start with verses that combat negative thoughts, behaviors, and situations you may be experiencing.

6. Show Daily Reverence to God - Start your day with prayer. Thank Him for His blessings, seek His guidance in decisions, and demonstrate His love through kind words and actions.

7. Reflect on the Following Scripture - Ask God to reveal its meaning and help you apply it to your life. *"Then Jesus said to his disciples, 'If any of you wants to be my follower, you must give up your own way, take up your cross, and follow me. If you try to hang on to your life, you will lose it. But if you give up your life for my sake, you will save it."* (New Living Translation, Matthew 16:24-25).

8. Connect with Other Believers - Join a church, get involved in ministry, or find ways to serve and grow in your community.

Cultivating a Space for Solitude

I'll be honest. I didn't always have a dedicated space to pray or just sit with God. For a long time, I prayed wherever I could, but as my relationship with Him grew, so did my desire to create a space that was just for us. That's when I made my very first *prayer closet*. Now, of course, you can talk to God anywhere— while you're driving, doing dishes, or even folding laundry. However, there's something incredibly powerful about having a spot where you can go intentionally to shut out the noise and just be with Him. When I step into my prayer closet, something shifts. The atmosphere is different. It's like I'm walking into a little sanctuary tucked away inside my home. Back when we lived in apartments, and space was tight, I used to retreat to the bathroom, close the door, block everything out, and get alone with God there. It wasn't fancy, but it worked. I met Him there.

Now that we're in our house, I've turned a walk-in closet into my prayer room. I've got my Bible, my journal, and a cozy bean bag chair. It's nothing extravagant, but it's mine. It's our space—a place where I can pour out my heart, be still, worship, cry, listen... just *be* with Him. It's peaceful. It's healing. It's holy. Honestly, I can't imagine life without it now. If you've never created a dedicated prayer space before, I want you to know that it doesn't have to be anything super fancy. Just make sure it is intentional. Even a corner in your room, a chair by the window, or a quiet space in your car during lunch breaks can become your sanctuary if your heart is open. The goal isn't perfection—it's presence.

God wants to meet with you, and He shows up when you make room for Him. In Matthew 6:6 (NLT), the Bible says, *"But when you pray, go away by yourself, shut the door behind you, and pray to your Father in private. Then your Father, who sees everything, will reward you."* Deuteronomy 8:3 reminds us, *"People do not live by bread alone; rather, we live by every word that comes from the mouth of the Lord."* We need more than food and success to feel whole—we need *Him*, every single day.

Creating space for God—both physically and mentally—isn't just a cute idea; it's a lifeline. It helps you tune out the noise, renew your mind, and truly focus on what matters. If we don't make intentional time for God, it's so easy to get lost in the busyness of life. We mistake movement for meaning. We chase productivity instead of purpose. We get caught in a whirlwind of "doing," and our connection with God feels distant before we know it. We have to ask ourselves, *Is my life postured toward me... or toward Him?*

Are we truly seeking His will, or are we just hoping He'll bless the plans we've already made? One of the enemy's sneakiest strategies isn't to lure us into sin; it's to keep us distracted, not with bad things but with *too many good things*. He'll keep us so busy that we're too tired to spend time with the One who gives us rest, so even if life feels "full" and your spirit is empty, that's your sign that it is time to make space. If you're reading this and realizing that life's been a blur—rushing from one role to the next (mom, wife, entrepreneur, professional, caretaker...)—I want you to pause. Take a breath. Ask yourself, *Am I making time for what truly matters?*

The Cultivated BOSS Method™ Tie-In: Bold in Faith

When we choose to *prioritize God*, everything else begins to align. We gain clarity, direction, and peace when we seek Him first. When we know our Creator, we start to understand our true identity. You can't walk in bold faith without knowing the One you're placing your trust in. That's why the first pillar of the Cultivated BOSS Method™ is Bold in Faith, because true confidence begins with intimacy. When you know your Creator personally, you stop doubting His plan and start trusting His character. Boldness doesn't mean having all the answers; it means knowing the One who does.

That's why I created my prayer closet, and it is why I'll never go back to the way things used to be. If you don't have a prayer space yet, I encourage you to start today. It doesn't have to be elaborate. It just has to be meaningful, just yours, and just His. To make it easier, I put together something for you. It is a free resource to help you create your own sacred space. Visit www.eyfbook.com to download the "Prayer Space Setup Guide" to help you build a sacred place for daily connection and intimacy with your Creator. You'll get a materials list, a step-by-step checklist, and custom prayers and prompts to guide your time with God. I promise that it's not just about setting up a space. It's about setting up your *life* to align with Him.

CHAPTER 2
UNDERSTAND YOUR PURPOSE AND CALLING

"For I know the plans I have for you," says the Lord. "They are plans for good and not for disaster, to give you a future and a hope."
(Jeremiah 29:11, NLT)

A Divine Detour: Ruth's Obedience in Uncertainty

Have you ever wondered: *Why am I here? What more does God have in store for me? Am I doing what God has called me to do?* Lately, I've noticed so many people asking themselves these very questions, yet they are unsure of where or how to start. I know exactly how that feels because I asked myself those same questions when I found myself without a job or acceptance into school. If you're feeling stuck or uncertain about your purpose right now, know that you're not alone. I've been there too, and in this chapter, I want to walk with you as you discover what God has in store for your life.

Before I go deeper into my story, I want to pause and reflect on a woman in the Bible who also experienced loss, uncertainty, and an unclear future—Ruth. She wasn't a leader or prophet. She was a widow who had just lost her husband. She had no children, no job, and no clear path forward. She had every reason to give up, but she chose obedience. She followed Naomi, her mother-in-law, into a foreign land and the unknown simply because she trusted Naomi's God. That one decision became the turning point for Ruth's life.

Now, imagine this for a moment. You're Ruth. You've just experienced deep loss. You're standing at a crossroads with no job, money, or certainty about the future. One path leads back to comfort and familiarity, and the other leads to a place where you've never been and where you'll have to trust God with each step. Ruth chose the latter. She said yes to God's plan without knowing the outcome.

> **●Real Talk Moment:**
> Obedience doesn't come with a GPS. Sometimes God just says *go*, and waits to see if you trust Him enough to move without a map.

Can you relate? Maybe you're in your own Moab moment—between what was and what could be. Maybe you're feeling the nudge to walk away from comfort and step into calling, even if you can't see the whole picture yet. Ruth didn't know she would meet Boaz. She didn't know she'd become the great-grandmother of King David or be included in the lineage of Jesus Christ. All she did was obey, and God did the rest.

The Hidden Start of a Bigger Assignment

Remember when I previously shared about finding myself without a job or acceptance into school? I'll never forget the moment I sat staring at my computer screen. My heart was pounding as I opened the email from the university I had planned to attend that month. The words, *"We regret to inform you,"* hit me like a ton of bricks. Honestly, I read that sentence at least three times, hoping it would magically change. I thought that maybe my screen was glitching and the "Congratulations!" email was still loading. *Lord, what is this about? I thought this was my chance to start anesthesia school?* I had no backup plan or means of earning an income, and at that moment, I felt lost, embarrassed, and completely unsure of what to do next.

Let me take you back to that moment. It was more than just a season of waiting—it was a defining season that reshaped my faith and purpose. This all took place over just a few months, from April through August. Months before I left my job at the pain clinic, I began feeling a strong desire to help women grow in their faith. I didn't know how it would unfold, but it wasn't going away. After I left the clinic in early April, that desire didn't go away; in fact, it grew louder. *Okay, God... but how?*

Around that time, I started thinking about ways to encourage women in their faith, and the idea of creating journals filled with scripture and words of affirmation came to mind. I put the idea into action and created a packet filled with information about who God is, how to discover your identity in Christ, what the attributes of God are, and who He is. I also designed custom notebooks for my younger sisters who were still figuring out their paths in life. These notebooks weren't anything fancy—I was just experimenting. I printed selfies and face shots of them and taped them to the front of each notebook. They looked like a cross between a school project and a Pinterest fail, but they were made with love and holy intention!

Then, we had a meeting where I gave them their notebooks, and we talked about what their purpose was, why they were here, who God said they are, and how He had uniquely called them. Let me tell you, I *felt* the fire of purpose burning inside me as I did that. They were encouraged, and so was I. What started as a creative project just for my sisters sparked something even deeper in me. It wasn't just about journals anymore. It was as if God was planting the first seed for a much bigger assignment, something that would eventually evolve into a book, a coaching program, and a full-circle moment I never saw coming.

Ruth didn't start out with a clear plan either. After arriving in Bethlehem, she humbly began gleaning leftover grain in the fields just to survive. What seemed like a small, mundane task was actually the very place where purpose met provision. Boaz, her future husband, saw her faithfulness, and God used that moment to begin rewriting her story. You never know how your obedience in the "small things" will lead to something far greater.

Over the next few weeks, I started researching how to take this further. I looked into creating custom journals, explored different materials, and even started checking out Cricut machines. I was excited, thinking maybe this was the direction in which God was leading me. Then, one day, while I was doing my usual internet surfing,

I suddenly felt the Holy Spirit speak to me. *"You're not creating journals. You're going to write a book."* Wait, what? *Write a book?* I literally stopped in my tracks. This was mind-blowing to me because I had *never, ever* had a desire to write a book. Right then and there, I knew this wasn't just some random thought—this was God speaking directly to me, but I couldn't help but wonder... *How could I turn my journal idea into an entire book?* Then, the questions started rolling in. *Lord, I don't even know how to write a book. Where would I even start?*

> 💬**Real Talk Moment:**
> God doesn't call the equipped, He equips the called. If you're waiting to feel qualified before you say yes, you'll miss the training ground of obedience.

If you've ever felt unqualified for what God is asking you to do, I want you to remember this. Ruth was a Moabite woman—an outsider. She was not even part of the chosen people, yet God hand-picked her to play a major role in the lineage of Jesus. That's how Divine purpose looks. It's not about qualifications—it's about availability. Your surrender is what positions you for impact.

I immediately switched my Google search from *how to create a journal* to *how to write a book.* One minute, I was researching paper quality, and the next, I was out here trying to figure out how to become the next *Priscilla Shirer.* God moves quickly! That search eventually led me to a woman who had written a book that helped aspiring authors write, self-publish, and launch their books in 90 days. I was so excited because I knew God had led me straight to her website. I bought her book and started reading, waiting on God to reveal more to me.

When Obedience Doesn't Make Sense

While still exploring ways to help women, I was also doing what most people do when they're in between jobs, applying for a new one. I applied for jobs—mostly in critical care—both as a nurse practitioner and as a registered nurse, so I could keep my critical care skills up, but *every single job I applied for had an issue.*

One position had amazing pay, but the previous nurse practitioner had already left, and no one was available to train me. That meant I'd basically be thrown into the role with no guidance, trying to figure everything out on my own. Another position seemed promising—I had even started orientation, but then, one of my sisters who was going to help us out with our kids could no longer help due to my husband and I's busy schedule demands. It felt like door after door was closing, and I was left asking God: *Why isn't anything working out?*

Maybe like Ruth or like me, you've had to leave behind comfort, familiarity, or even a career that once felt secure. Sometimes, purpose requires us to release something before fully understanding what God is doing. That's the faith walk. Ruth had no idea she was walking toward Boaz—she was simply being obedient. Don't despise the field you're currently planted in, even if it doesn't look like the harvest yet. God may be using this exact season to prepare you for what's next.

> **🗨Real Talk Moment:**
> Purpose and calling don't always look glamorous. Sometimes, they look like picking up scraps, staying faithful, and trusting that God is still writing your story.

Then, one night, God sent me a dream.

A Dream and a Divine Warning

Now, to make a long story short, in the dream, I was working at my kids' school, but my daughter's teacher and I weren't getting along. This wasn't her real teacher, but a random woman who had accused me of something I hadn't done. Ma'am... in *my* own dream? *The audacity.* I knew I was being wrongfully accused, so I decided to quit the job and leave. On my way out the door, my husband was walking with me as I walked into the parking lot. We were discussing what my next move would be, and I started thinking about getting on a nursing contract. *Maybe that's what I should do,* I thought. *Maybe I should lock in a contract and start working again.* Then, suddenly, the dream shifted. I found myself looking at a white screen. At the top of the screen, bold words appeared:

"DON'T WORK RIGHT NOW." Then, underneath that heading, six or so words started falling, stacking on top of each other. They were dropping so fast, and as each word landed, I heard a distinct clank, clank, clank. It was almost like metal hitting metal. The words were moving too quickly for me to catch them all, but I remember one word clearly: "Foreclosed." After all the words had stacked up on the screen, a final message came crashing down and *smashed* everything underneath it. "DON'T LET YOUR JOB WITHDRAW YOU FROM YOUR MUSCLE WORK."

I shot up in bed. The message felt so familiar, like God had already told me this before, just maybe in a different way. It was as if He was repeating Himself, trying to get my attention. It was almost like He was saying, "Daughter, do I have to spell it out for you? Do not work right now." I immediately told my husband because he's the first person I go to when something out of the ordinary happens. He was amazed, too. At that moment, I knew. God had something bigger in store for me, something greater than the positions I kept applying for. He didn't want me distracted by chasing after jobs that weren't in alignment with His plan. He wanted me to draw closer to Him, to get deeper into His Word, and to prepare myself for the new season He was leading me into. When I woke up, I looked up the definition of *foreclose. It* means to rule out or prevent a course of action. I had been trying so hard to make something work, but God was making Himself clear: *This is not the path I have for you.* This message wasn't just about employment; it was a wake-up call from God, reminding me not to let the demands of a job pull me away from the real work He had called me to do. My *muscle work* was the purpose He had placed inside me—the calling to help women discover their identity in Christ and walk boldly in their God-given purpose. It was clear that this season wasn't about working for a paycheck but building what God had ordained for me from the start. I didn't know all the details at that time, but one thing was certain. My journey was about to change in a way I never expected. All of my dreams—every vision, every encounter—were documented in the Notes section on my phone. I had this particular dream on June 9th.

> **🗨Real Talk Moment:**
> Just because the job pays doesn't mean it aligns. Don't trade purpose for a paycheck. One feeds your wallet, the other fuels your soul.

When God Opens Doors, Only He Can Open

Shortly after that dream, something unexpected happened. The same woman from whom I had purchased the book was offering a free workshop titled, "How to Write a Book That Builds Your Brand." Without hesitation, I signed up. I couldn't help but think, *Wow, God, You are truly equipping me with everything I need.* Toward the end of her online workshop, she extended an invitation for all who attended to join her Boot Camp, and it wasn't just any program. This was a comprehensive, 12-month experience designed to help you write, self-publish, and launch your book, but it didn't stop there. It also taught how to design your book for marketing, plan effective promotion and sales campaigns, and build a thought leadership brand. That night, I went straight into prayer. I said, "God, if it's Your will for me to actually write this book, show me a sign that this is truly what You want me to do." A few days later, as I was getting ready for bed, that sign came—louder and clearer than I ever expected. I remember falling asleep, and not long after, I was suddenly awakened. As my eyes opened, something startled me. There, floating up in the air on the side of my bed, was a miniature green tree, about the size of a small lamp. The tree had red fruit on it, and it was slowly moving closer to me, as if to give me a good look. My eyes were glued to it. I blinked a million times, trying to make sure what I was seeing was real. Then, just as suddenly as it had appeared, it vanished. I couldn't believe what I had just experienced. My husband was at work that night—he works night shifts—so I couldn't wait to tell him first thing in the morning. Deep down, I knew what this encounter meant. This was God confirming what He had placed in front of me to do. The tree, full of fruit, was His way of showing me that this assignment would bear good fruit. This Divine confirmation happened on July 16th. So much had happened in just a few short months, and I was finally beginning to see how God was ordering my steps all along.

Okay, just to give you an idea of the timing of everything: I left my position at the pain clinic at the beginning of April. In May, I received my rejection letter from the university, and that's when I began applying for jobs, both NP and RN roles in critical care. One job after another began to fall through. In June, God gave me a dream that revealed I wasn't supposed to return to work just yet. In mid-July, I received confirmation to pursue writing a book, and I joined the book-writing program, officially starting my journey toward authorship. Then in August, I would find myself applying to anesthesia school for a third time, still seeking clarity, but also beginning to see how God was reshaping my path.

Now that I had my confirmation, I hit another obstacle—finances. The boot camp was a 12-month program with a monthly fee. I didn't know how I was going to afford it. I went back to God in prayer again. I prayed, "Okay, God. I need your help supplying the finances. I don't know how this is going to happen. My husband already has so much on his plate." A couple of days after that prayer, I received a phone call from my mom. She had no idea what I was trying to do, and by that point, I hadn't worked in about four months. We started with some small talk, and then, out of nowhere, she said something that left me speechless. "I have some money I want to give you," she said. My mouth dropped open. "What? How come?" I asked her, "Why now, out of all the days?" I just knew God was in the mix, but I wanted to hear what she would say. She simply responded, "I don't know. I just thought about it." LOL! This is how God works! He'll place things on our hearts, and sometimes, we're not even sure where the ideas come from, but that's the Holy Spirit nudging us, working behind the scenes. With my mom and dad giving me this unexpected blessing, we had half of what we needed to cover the monthly fee for 12 months. Then, my husband stepped in and said he would cover the other half. Look at God! God wasn't done yet! It was like heaven had *Amazon Prime*-ed my blessings, right on time and fully funded. The following month, out of nowhere, my husband received a raise at work. I couldn't believe how smoothly everything was falling into place. I'm telling you, God is good, and when He says, "It's your time," it's your time! When it's your season, God will open doors that no one else can, and you'll know it without a doubt.

> 🗨**Real Talk Moment**:
> God doesn't need your resume, He needs your yes. Let Him be the CEO of your next chapter, and you just follow the Spirit-led calendar invites.

Over time, I realized that the answers to my questions became clear when I stayed connected to God. The truth is, God can use us *anywhere* and at *any time*. You'll feel the gentle nudge of the Holy Spirit—almost like a warm embrace—when it's time for a change. Sometimes, however, you might feel the opposite instead of peace— an unsettling feeling in your spirit. This discomfort can show up as restlessness, frustration, or a deep sense that something just isn't right where you are. That unsettling feeling isn't something to ignore; it's often God's way of signaling that He's preparing you for something new. It's a holy discomfort meant to stir you into action, prompting you to seek His guidance and step into the next season He's calling you to. It's up to us to recognize these moments, obey, and move in alignment with God's will. If you ever find yourself feeling lost or confused about what God is trying to do in your life, don't worry. You're not alone. Those moments of uncertainty are often the doorway to discovering your *true* purpose and calling. Stay connected to God, remain sensitive to His voice, and trust that He will lead you exactly where you're meant to be. Your calling isn't just about what you *do*—it's about *who* you become as you walk in obedience and allow God to shape your journey. Whether that door opens again or not, I now understand that purpose is not about chasing roles, it's about staying rooted in God's will. *What's one desire you've been holding onto that you need to place back in God's hands?*

Ruth's story teaches us that destiny doesn't always show up with a grand entrance. It often enters quietly, through Divine appointments, closed doors, and unlikely encounters. If you're reading this and wondering why certain things didn't work out or why God rerouted your steps, let Ruth's journey remind you of this promise. He sees the whole picture. He's positioning you for a future that carries legacy, impact, and eternal significance.

> 🗨**Real Talk Moment**:
> You're not being overlooked, you're being positioned. The delay isn't denial, it's Divine alignment.

The Cultivated BOSS Method™ Tie-In: Bold in Faith

Discovering your purpose is powerful, but walking in it requires bold faith. Sometimes God gives you glimpses before clarity, but it's your faith that carries you through the in-between. Bold faith means saying "yes" even when the door hasn't opened yet. Ruth didn't need certainty. She just needed courage, and so do you.

Discover Clarity in Your Purpose and Calling

Before we dive into how to discover your purpose and calling, let's clarify something important—the difference between the two. Your purpose is your "why." It's the reason you were created. It's rooted in God's plan for you to love Him, serve others, and reflect His glory. Your calling, on the other hand, is the unique "how." It's God's specific path, assignment, or role to fulfill that purpose in different seasons of your life. Think of it like this. Your purpose is the foundation, but your calling is the house built on top. Your calling may shift—teacher today, coach tomorrow, entrepreneur next year, but your purpose remains the same. You are designed to live for God and impact others through your obedience.

Aligning Your Desires with God's Direction

Here are a few strategies to help you gain clarity on your purpose and calling.

1. Reflect on your heart's desires – Ask yourself: *Do my goals, dreams, and daily decisions align with what God desires for my life?* Write down any areas where your desires may need to shift or surrender.

2. Pray for revelation – Spend intentional time in prayer, asking God if there's something He wants to reveal to you. Sometimes, the answers we're searching for are just one prayer away.

3. Write down what God reveals – Keep a journal nearby during prayer. Record any thoughts, scriptures, or nudges that stir your spirit and ask God to show you the next step.

4. Take obedient action – Faith comes alive through action. Start with one small step God has placed on your heart, and trust Him to open the next door.

5. Reflect on your current role – Ask yourself: *Do I feel called here?* If not, pray for either contentment where you are or clarity to step into what's next.

6. Show up with excellence – Serve faithfully where you are. *"Work willingly at whatever you do, as though you were working for the Lord..."* (Colossians 3:23–24, NLT)

Clarity Follows Obedience

> 💬**Real Talk Moment**:
> You can't fulfill your calling on clarity alone. You have to move at some point, even if all you've got is a mustard seed of courage.

Remember, we can make our own plans, but it's the Lord who ordains our steps. We don't seek the gift. We seek the Giver. Proverbs 16:3 (NLT) says: *"Commit your actions to the Lord, and your plans will succeed."* Understanding your purpose and identifying the roles you're called to is essential because it allows you to partner with God and actively participate in His divine plan for your life. Visit www.eyfbook.com to download the "Purpose & Calling Discovery Template" to help you clarify your unique calling and align your life with God's divine purpose.

CHAPTER 3
RECOGNIZE THAT YOU ARE ROYALTY

> *"The Lord will hold you in his hand for all to see— a splendid crown in the hand of God."*
> **– (Isaiah 62:3, NLT)**

Meet Deborah: A True Portrait of Godly Royalty

Before we dive into my story, I want to introduce you to a woman in the Bible whose life paints a powerful picture of what it means to walk in royalty. Her name is Deborah.

Deborah wasn't born into wealth or nobility and didn't have a fancy title, yet she embodied true, God-ordained royalty. She was a prophetess, a judge, and a leader of Israel during one of the most oppressive times in the nation's history (Judges 4–5). While others hid in fear, Deborah stood boldly in her Divine identity. She didn't just speak on behalf of God. She led armies into battle when no one else had the courage. She sat under the Palm of Deborah, offering wisdom, settling disputes, and guiding her people with clarity and grace.

What set Deborah apart wasn't her circumstances. It was her obedience, boldness, and unwavering connection to God. She wasn't intimidated by what others might have thought. She didn't need a crown to lead. She simply answered the call, and the land had peace for 40 years through her obedience.

> **🗩Real Talk Moment:**
> Stop waiting for a title, platform, or applause to walk in what God already called you to do. If He appointed you, He'll anoint you.

As you read this chapter, keep Deborah's story in the back of your mind. She is a reminder that you don't need to wait for someone to call you worthy. You already are. You don't have to wait until you feel qualified. You're already chosen. Royalty isn't about outward status. It's about knowing who you are in Christ and walking in that identity daily.

Caught Up in the Hype

There was a time in my life when I let other people's thoughts and opinions determine my worth. I would shift how I acted just to fit in, molding myself into who I thought others wanted me to be. I clung to relationships that had long expired, holding on simply to avoid feeling alone, even when those connections no longer served me or reflected who I truly was. I allowed situations at work or in my personal life to dictate my mood and control how my day would unfold. Without realizing it, I was operating in the flesh, and my spiritual light was dim—on the verge of going out.

> **🗩Real Talk Moment:**
> When your flesh leads, your faith dims. The enemy doesn't need to destroy you if he can distract you long enough to forget who you are.

When I reflect on that time, I think about how different I was from the woman God created me to be. I wasn't walking in my royalty. I was walking in confusion, insecurity, and compromise. Then I remember women like Deborah, who didn't let the noise of culture or fear of judgment stop her from walking in her God-given authority. She stood tall in her identity, even in a time when women weren't expected to lead.

I remember when my life revolved around the nightlife, partying like there was no tomorrow. Most nights of the week, you could find me out with my friends, fully convinced that I was "living my best life." Back then, it felt exciting, even freeing. There was a rush in planning out an entire day around getting ready to hit the bar or the club. Sometimes, the entire day became a full-blown event. Suppose it was someone's birthday, a holiday, or a big night out. In that case, we'd start early with a trip to the mall to find the perfect outfit, which basically meant trying on ten things we couldn't afford, buying one of them anyway, and then pretending it wasn't cutting into next week's bill money.

Then came the hours spent preparing: hair done, nails on point, makeup flawless—every detail had to be just right. The excitement would build as everything came together, and by the time I did my final mirror check, I felt untouchable. I thought I looked "bomb." I mean, if confidence could take you to heaven, I'd have been first in line, dressed to the nines. My hair was styled to perfection, my makeup was on point, and my outfit had me feeling like I was on top of the world. In those moments, no one could tell me I wasn't *cute*. I felt unstoppable. Before heading out, we'd always make a quick stop at the liquor store because the drinks at the club were way too expensive, and we were balling on a budget. It became part of the whole preparation experience, the final piece of what I thought was the perfect night out. Our plan was always the same—buy one or two drinks at most once we got to the spot. Once we were feeling good, it was time to hit the party scene. I remember us standing outside the club, rain or shine, waiting in line to get in. Our heels were aching, and our makeup was slowly melting, but still trying to act like we were fine. You could hear the bass thumping from outside. The music was so loud that it practically pulled you in, and if your favorite song happened to come on while you were still waiting... oh, it was over—the party would start right there on the sidewalk. Once we made it inside, we would dive straight into the energy of the crowd—loud music, packed dance floor, bodies moving everywhere. The DJ controlled the vibe of the entire place. One song could completely shift the atmosphere. If the DJ dropped a beat that hyped the girls up, you'd see all kinds of shaking and moving going on, a bunch of gyrating all over the Lord's land, as some old folks would say. If it were a song that insinuated something sexual, the dance floor would turn into a scene of grinding and movements that left little to the imagination. The whole mood would shift if the DJ dared to play a song that glorified violence or fighting. People would get hyped and start jumping around, and sometimes, it didn't stop there. Fights would break out. Do you know what the sad part was? I knew exactly which songs were likely to set it off. I'd think to myself, *The DJ better cut this off before somebody starts swinging.* Like clockwork, chaos would erupt. People would be shouting and shoving, and sometimes, things would get much worse. Eventually, the DJ would cut the music off and say, *"Party's over."* I remember my friends saying, *"We can never go anywhere and just have fun!"* What was the hard truth? We had no business being in those places to begin with.

Looking back, I realize I wasn't myself when I drank. I know I'm not alone in that realization—*liquid courage* is real. It makes you bold in ways you wouldn't normally be, especially when you've had too much. I remember one night when a song came on that fueled something dark inside me. The lyrics stirred up anger and hostility toward everyone who wasn't part of my crew. I caught myself vibing to the beat, mean-mugging strangers, and bobbing my head like I *wanted* someone to test me. I was on *Go Mode* and didn't care what the outcome would be. The truth is that the kingdom of darkness was influencing me. When I reflect on those moments now, it's clear that if we're not living for the Kingdom of God, we're serving another kingdom, and that's the kingdom of darkness. There's no in-between.

Escaping the Club Scene, But Still Far from God

At that time in my life, I didn't see the club scene as a distraction from God. I saw it as my time to have fun and live my life while God remained at a distance, *waiting for me to turn it around.* I had gone out the night before. I was out late into the *wee hours* of the morning, but I still got up for church that Sunday. We were sitting in service when it hit me. I had gone with my older sister, someone who always looked out for me and still does to this day in different ways. We were listening to the pastor preach when she suddenly leaned over and whispered, "I can smell the alcohol on you." My eyes shot open wide, and I wanted to disappear right there in that pew. I tried to hold my breath and breathe as little as possible for the rest of the service, convinced everyone around me could smell my Saturday night breath. At one point, I thought I was going to pass out and meet Jesus early. I thought I was going to be carried out of church on a stretcher due to the lack of oxygen to my brain. That moment stuck with me. It made me realize how far I had drifted from God. Even though I was physically sitting in His house, mentally and spiritually, I couldn't have been further away. My body was present, but my heart and spirit were lost, tangled up in a life pulling me further from Him. Eventually, I left the club scene behind. I woke up and realized that my life of partying wasn't leading me anywhere except right into the hands of the enemy. *I left the club scene, but I still wasn't making time for God.*

> 🎤**Real Talk Moment:**
> You can leave a lifestyle behind and still miss your calling if you don't fill that empty space with God. Busyness in the name of success is still bondage if it pulls you from His presence.

Even though I had walked away from one distraction, I found myself still operating in the flesh, just in a different way. Early on in my career, I finally started making good money, but instead of using it wisely, I spent it just as fast as I earned it—like the paycheck had an expiration date. I spent it on food, clothes, and trips. I even tithed occasionally, but deep down, I thought, *This is my time to stack up and secure my future.* The only thing I ended up stacking was debt. I was working hard just to stay broke, and I didn't even realize it. That's exactly how the enemy works. His goal isn't always to tempt us with obvious sin. Sometimes, his goal is to just keep us busy enough with distractions, even *good* things, so we don't have any time left for God.

Growing up, I was that little girl who practically lived outside, riding my bike, hanging out at the park, and getting into neighborhood fights with kids who thought they could bully me or mess with my older sister. At the time, my younger sisters weren't even born, so it was just my older sister and me holding it down. Growing up, we spent a lot of time hanging out at my grandparents' house, the official family hangout spot. With ten kids (five girls and five boys), my grandparents' home was always buzzing with activity. I have a ton of cousins, so there was never a dull moment. My Granny, the proud matriarch of our family on my mom's side, still holds it all together at 86 years old. God rest my granddad's soul, he helped build the foundation of love and legacy that made their home the heartbeat of our family gatherings. To this day, my cousins still laugh and remind me of how *bad* I was back then, especially the older cousins, since they were the ones babysitting us. As I grew into my late teens and early twenties, I learned to walk away from confrontations more often. However, if someone pushed me too far, that switch would flip, and I'd become someone completely different. I remember getting into heated arguments that left me so angry that it literally blurred my vision. If you've ever heard someone say, "I was so angry I couldn't see straight," let me tell you, that's real. Here's the truth. In those moments of anger and rage, we have to remember *who we are* and *who we represent*. As Christians, we are disciples of Christ—*followers of Jesus*. When we allow our flesh to take over, we stop representing the Kingdom of God and instead operate under the influence of the kingdom of darkness.

Even as I slowly left behind that lifestyle, I didn't fully recognize my value. I didn't yet understand that God had already declared me royalty, just like He did with Deborah. What I love about Deborah's story is that she didn't need the world's approval to step into her role. She was already chosen and already appointed. She didn't let the expectations of others determine whether or not she would lead. That's what I was still learning. I needed to see myself the way God already saw me.

Reigniting the Light Within

I remember those days of drinking and partying, thinking I was just having fun and living life. Every time we indulge in the things of this world, our spiritual lights dim more and more. The human body is made up of three parts: body, soul, and spirit. Back then, I let my flesh—my body—take the lead, and my soul—my mind and emotions—suffered as a result. My fleshly desires shaped my thoughts, feelings, and actions. When we let our flesh lead, it pulls us down a path toward *death,* but when we allow our spirit—our true, God-given self—to lead, it becomes a path toward *life*. The Holy Spirit speaks directly to our spirit, but when there's too much noise—distractions, emotional burdens, or the weight of our past—we can't hear Him clearly. That's why solitude with God is essential. It allows us to quiet our souls and hear His voice. Every time we indulge in the things of this world, our spiritual lights dim more and more.

Now, your light may not have dimmed the same way mine did. Maybe it wasn't partying or drinking. Maybe it was having toxic relationships, overworking yourself to exhaustion, constantly seeking validation from others, or drowning in anxiety and fear. No matter the cause, anything that pulls you away from God's presence will dim your light.

Let's be honest. As career-driven women, we sometimes get so caught up in chasing success that we start ignoring our true identity. We stay busy climbing the ladder and checking off achievements, but we forget that we are royalty, chosen by God. We need to lead ourselves like Deborah led the people of Israel with confidence, courage, and clarity.

Deborah didn't wait for someone else to give her permission to lead. She didn't seek validation from people. Her boldness came from her connection to God. She sat under her palm tree and judged wisely because she was Spirit-led. When the time came to step up and fight, she didn't hesitate. She led an entire army into battle because she believed in what God had said, not what culture expected.

That's the kind of leadership we need in our own lives, especially when the enemy tries to whisper lies about who we are. Just like Deborah, we have to know our authority in Christ and act like it.

We forget that our actions, mindset, and priorities should reflect that royal position. Being too busy for God is a subtle way of handing the enemy the victory, but the beautiful truth is that *you can reclaim that light*. Walking in the royalty God has called you to isn't just about knowing who you are; it's about living like you believe it. It requires action, intention, and daily choices that reflect your identity as a daughter of the King.

The Cultivated BOSS Method™ Tie-In: Bold in Faith

Walking in royalty begins with bold faith. Deborah didn't wait for outside validation. She moved with confidence because she trusted the God who called her. That's what Bold in Faith is all about: moving forward even when you don't feel qualified, because you know

Who qualified you. You are royalty, not because of your résumé, but because of your relationship with the King.

Strategies to Reclaim Your Light and Walk in Royalty

Here are some strategies to help you start reclaiming your light and stepping fully into the woman God has called you to be.

1. See Yourself as a New Creation. – Remind yourself daily that you are a new creation, adopted into God's family through the blood of Jesus. Start each morning by declaring, "I am made new, loved, and chosen by God."

2. Acknowledge Your Inheritance. – Write down 6 things you've inherited as a child of God, such as peace, joy, strength, authority, love, and eternal life. Reflect on these blessings daily and thank God for each one.

3. Replace Old Habits with Scripture. – Identify negative habits like anger, jealousy, or people-pleasing, and find scriptures that directly counteract those struggles. Whenever those habits arise, speak the scripture aloud and redirect your focus back to God's truth.

4. Follow God's Commandments Daily. – Each day, ask yourself, *What can I do today to honor God's commandments?* Then take intentional action, whether it's showing kindness, offering forgiveness, or loving someone who's hard to love.

5. Accept That You Are Called and Chosen. – Affirm every day that you are called and chosen by God for a specific purpose. Walk confidently in that truth, knowing He has set you apart to fulfill a Divine assignment.

6. Reframe Your Mindset in Weak Moments. – When you catch yourself slipping, declare out loud, "I choose to live for the Kingdom of God, not the kingdom of darkness." Then remove yourself from the situation and refocus your mind on God's calling for your life.

7. Reflect God's Royalty in the Workplace. – Maintain a positive attitude, treat colleagues with respect, and handle challenges with integrity. Whether it's navigating office politics, meeting dead-

lines, or dealing with difficult coworkers, always respond in a way that reflects Christ's character.

8. When faced with challenges at work, take a deep breath before responding, pray for wisdom, and choose words that reflect grace rather than frustration. – Approach every task, big or small, with diligence, integrity, and a mindset that says, *I am working as if for the Lord, not just for people* (Colossians 3:23, NIV).

Living Like Royalty Every Day

We have to be mindful of the places we go and the environments in which we allow ourselves to be. Know that you were created in God's image—holy, righteous, and perfectly designed. You are His masterpiece, and your light should shine brightly no matter what your circumstances are. *"So God created human beings in His own image. In the image of God He created them; male and female He created them."* (Genesis 1:27, NLT)

In today's busy world, especially for career-driven women, it's so easy to get so caught up in work, success, and everyday responsibilities that we forget who we are in Christ. We run ourselves into exhaustion, thinking productivity equals worth, while ignoring the fact that we are royalty and should behave as such. Deborah reminds us that we are *not ordinary*. We are divinely called and spiritually equipped to lead with wisdom, speak with authority, and live with bold faith. Just like Deborah, you don't need to wait for someone to hand you a crown. You already wear one. You just have to start living like it.

💬Real Talk Moment:
The world runs on burnout. The Kingdom runs on overflow.

To stay rooted in your identity as royalty, take time each day to reflect on who God says you are. Visit www.eyfbook.com to download the "Rooted and Royalty Worksheet" to help you walk confidently in your royal identity as a daughter of the King.

CHAPTER 4

DELIVERANCE AND SPIRITUAL WARFARE

"For we are not fighting against flesh and blood enemies, but against evil rulers and authorities of the unseen world, against mighty Powers in this dark world, and against evil spirits in the heavenly places."
(Ephesians 6:12, NLT)

The Power of Deliverance: Mary Magdalene's Redemption Story

Before we dive into spiritual warfare and mindset, I want to introduce you to a woman from Scripture who experienced true spiritual freedom through deliverance. Her name was Mary Magdalene. The Bible tells us in Luke 8:2 that she had been afflicted by seven demons, tormented, oppressed, and likely misunderstood by society. Imagine the mental, emotional, and spiritual bondage she must have endured. Yet, when she encountered Jesus, everything changed. He cast out every unclean spirit and restored her fully. Mary didn't just receive freedom; she became a follower of Christ, one of the first to witness His resurrection, and a bold witness of His power.

Her transformation shows us something deeply personal: God is not afraid of your past. He is not limited by your mistakes, your battles, or even the demons you've been carrying. When Mary encountered Jesus, He didn't shame her. He spoke life into her. His deliverance wasn't just a moment; it was a complete redirection. He called her forward into purpose, destiny, and intimacy with Him, and Woman of God, He can do the same for you. If you walk by faith and believe, God can speak directly into your life, too. He wants to deliver to you, speak to your heart, and send you on assignment, just like He did with Mary Magdalene. You don't have to be perfect, just willing. You serve a God who sees you fully and chooses you anyway.

> **🗩Real Talk Moment:**
> Some of us are waiting to be worthy enough for freedom, but Jesus already called you worthy when He died for you. Walk like you're chosen.

When the Unseen Becomes Seen: A Wake-Up Call to Spiritual Warfare

Have you ever felt like there's more going on around you than what you can see? That's because there is. We are constantly surrounded by an unseen spiritual realm, and whether we realize it or not, we're in the middle of a battle—spiritual warfare. However, let's be clear. This war isn't against people; it's against the enemy. Satan and his forces operate in the shadows, using deception, temptation, and strongholds to keep us bound. The Bible clarifies in Ephesians 6:12 (NLT) that our battle isn't against people. It's against the spiritual forces of darkness. The enemy's goal is to keep us trapped, distracted, and disconnected from God's purpose for our lives. Spiritual warfare is the ongoing battle between good and evil, where the enemy works to oppose God's will in our lives through temptation, oppression, and deception.

Let's be honest. One of the ways he does this is through toxic relationships. Most of us have found ourselves caught in situations where we knew something wasn't right, but we just couldn't walk away for some reason. God is still delivering women today just like He did for Mary Magdalene. I'll never forget what God showed me in the spirit realm concerning one of my sisters who was in a toxic relationship years ago. One night, I was fast asleep when I had a dream that felt so vivid, I knew it was more than just a dream; it was a revelation. In the dream, I saw my sister and her boyfriend. They had been together for years, but they weren't pouring into each other and weren't growing or thriving. They were stuck—trapped in stagnation. As I sat with them, I began speaking truth into their lives, telling them that there was so much more than this cycle in which they were caught up. I told them directly that they needed to separate, so they could grow individually and step into who God had called them to be. I was giving them the speech of a lifetime, encouraging them and pushing them to seek better for themselves. It was like I was fighting for their freedom, not physically, but spiritually. God was revealing to me what needed to take place between the two of them in the natural realm, and the enemy did not want it to manifest. The enemy wanted to keep them bound in dysfunction, preventing them from stepping into God's best plan for their lives, but through my dream, God was making His will known to me.

In the dream, they both seemed open to what I was saying. It was as if they understood that they needed to go their separate ways in order to truly grow and become who they were meant to be, but what happened next shook me to my core. As I started waking up, I felt my body begin to tremble—a sensation I've come to recognize whenever I'm transitioning into the spirit realm. It's like my body was shifting from the physical to the spiritual. I opened my eyes, and what I saw standing right over me made my heart nearly stop. There, on my bed, was a short, shadowy figure. It was a dark, faceless form—an unclean spirit—a demon. It stood at about the height of a young child, but there was nothing innocent about it. There was just darkness. I could feel its presence radiating anger as if it were absolutely furious about what I had just done in my dream. It didn't speak, but its body language said everything. It leaned in toward my face, raising a long, skinny finger and wagging it back and forth like a silent warning. All I could think was, *if this thing touches me, I'm swinging—even if I miss and hit air.* If I had to put words to what it was trying to say, it would be something like, *"I don't know what you think you're trying to do, but you can't have this couple. They belong to me."* I was frozen and terrified. I had never experienced anything like that before. It stood there for maybe ten seconds, shaking its head at me as if to say, *"You better back off."* In my mind, I began silently calling on Jesus, not even sure if I could get the words out loud. It was like my spirit knew what to do even though my body was paralyzed in fear. Then, just as suddenly as it appeared, it leaped off my bed and ran straight out of the bedroom. I sat up, my heart pounding in disbelief. I had never seen anything like that before. The kitchen light was on, casting a glow onto the wall outside our bedroom door. Then, I saw a shadow approaching. My stomach dropped. *Was it coming back?* As the shadow stepped closer, I tensed up, only to realize my husband was walking in from the hallway. At the time, he was in school because he was working toward his bachelor's degree in nursing, and he had to leave early for his clinical rotation, which was a couple of hours away. The moment I saw him, I blurted out, "Did you see that?! Did you see it run out of the room?!" He looked at me, confused. "See what?" Still shaken, I tried to explain. "There was a demonic figure standing on the bed, right over me. It jumped off and ran out of here!" Then, I told him about the dream I had right before it happened.

I love my husband so much because even though it sounded crazy, he didn't question me for a second. He just looked at me and said, "Pray." I just stared at him, thinking, *Pray? That's all you have to offer me at a time like this? Sir... I need holy oil, a priest, a cross, and a Bible, not just a one-word response and a goodbye wave!* At this point, I was ready to grab the kids, all their stuff, and my oversized suitcase purse (that's what my husband calls it because I can fit just about anything in it) and go stay with my parents until further notice.

My mind was racing. I had no idea back then that prayer is actually the most powerful weapon we have. To make matters worse, he was about to walk out the door, leaving the kids and me there alone. That realization made me even more terrified. Despite the storm of fearful thoughts flooding my mind, I prayed. I prayed for my sister and her boyfriend individually, their relationship, and for myself and my household. At the time, our son Noah was just a baby. He was sleeping beside me, and our daughter, Neoki, who was about three, was down the hall in her room. Before my husband left, I grabbed Neoki so they could both be in bed with me. I needed them close to me. At that point, I would've put the whole family in one bed, plus the dog (if we had one), a flashlight, and every nightlight in the house. I had no shame in my survival strategy. I needed to see them to know they were safe. I didn't know if that thing was returning, and I wasn't about to take any chances. Later that day, I immediately called my sister to tell her everything—the dream, the demon, all of it. She was floored. She was completely in disbelief. Honestly, I couldn't blame her.

I always knew there was a spirit realm around us, but actually *seeing* something from it was totally unexpected. That was undeniable proof that it exists. The actual moment happened so fast that I didn't even think about it, but as Christians, we have full power and authority to rebuke unclean spirits in the name of Jesus. It wasn't until later, after learning more about spiritual warfare, that I realized what was really going on. That spirit had been working behind the scenes to keep my sister and her boyfriend in bondage, and they had no idea. This was my first visual encounter with the spirit realm, but I've come to understand that these battles are happening all around us every single day. That's why we have to stay spiritually equipped. We may not always *see* what we're up against, but that doesn't mean the fight isn't real. Every day, we need to put on our spiritual armor because we're battling forces beyond what our eyes can perceive. God chooses who and what He wants to reveal, and when He does, we have to be ready for spiritual battle, whether we see it coming or not.

Deliverance Isn't Just for the Bible Days, It's for You Too

In the same way Mary Magdalene was once bound by demonic oppression before she encountered Jesus, my sister was also being spiritually held back in a relationship that wasn't aligned with God's will. Just as Jesus saw Mary's affliction and set her free, God was showing me through my dream that deliverance was needed, not just from a person, but from the spiritual strongholds that kept them both stuck. Mary Magdalene didn't just *get better*; she was freed, and that's what God wants for every woman walking in cycles of dysfunction. Deliverance starts with revelation and ends in transformation.

That demonic spirit I saw was undeniable proof that there is more happening around us than what we can see. And we don't have to be afraid. We have been given the authority to rebuke the enemy in Jesus's name. Just like Mary was set free by Jesus's power, you too can rise in boldness and shut the door to every unclean thing trying to hold you back.

Subtle Attacks, Supernatural Authority

Life gets busy. Between careers, relationships, family, and the never-ending to-do lists, it's easy to push God further and further down our priority list. We convince ourselves that we'll pray later. We'll study when we have more time and get serious about our spiritual walk after we reach the next career milestone or life goal, but the enemy doesn't wait. When we take our eyes off God, even for what seem like good reasons—chasing success, handling responsibilities, focusing on self-improvement—the enemy sees an opportunity to creep into our lives unnoticed. Slowly but surely, he influences our thoughts, emotions, and decisions, leading us down a path of exhaustion, dissatisfaction, and spiritual numbness.

> 💬**Real Talk Moment:**
> The enemy doesn't need a grand entrance. Sometimes all he needs is your exhaustion and your excuses.

Over the past few years, I've had recurring dreams of delivering people from unclean spirits. At first, I didn't think much of it, but the more it kept happening, the more I wanted to understand what it meant. I began to realize that God was revealing something deeper. He was showing me an area in which He wanted me to seek more knowledge and grow in. That curiosity led me down a path of learning about obtaining deliverance, participating in spiritual warfare, and breaking strongholds over my own life. I started doing self-deliverance, which is when believers take authority in Christ to break the enemy's power and make him flee (Luke 10:19, NLT). Strongholds are anything in our lives that go against the Word of God. They're lies from the enemy that keep us stuck in harmful thought patterns or habits we can't seem to shake. Subsequently, I began going into my prayer closet—I still do to this day—and renouncing anything negative: toxic behaviors, emotions, and even negative words spoken over me, but I didn't just stop there. I replaced those empty spaces with the fruits of the Holy Spirit: love, joy, peace, patience, kindness, goodness, faithfulness, gentleness, and self-control (Galatians 5:22-23, NLT). Obedience to God's Word is key, so I also took it a step further and started seeking out courses on spiritual warfare and deliverance. The prophetess who led one of my classes even did a detailed deliverance on me, and let me tell you, it put my relationship with God into overdrive.

Spiritual Warfare in the Workplace

I loved working as an agency nurse and doing 12-week contracts. It gave me the opportunity to float around to different hospitals and facilities, which meant I never had to stay anywhere longer than I wanted once my contract was up. There were plenty of places where I absolutely loved working, so much so that I'd stay for a while, and the staff would forget I was an agency nurse because I became part of their work family, lol. Then, there were places where I couldn't wait to leave, like one hospital where I felt the spirit of divination heavy in the atmosphere. A spirit of divination operates through manipulation, deception, and counterfeit wisdom. It often works through cliques, power-hungry leadership, and an atmosphere of exclusion, and that's exactly what I experienced there. The culture was cliquish, and if you weren't part of the "in crowd," you were basically left to fend for yourself. You'd think we were back in high school, minus the lockers and with a lot more patients and IV poles.

That sense of exclusion mirrors what Mary Magdalene may have felt before Jesus delivered her, isolated, judged, and labeled. Once Jesus restored her, her identity changed. She wasn't bound by rejection anymore; she was commissioned for a purpose. Her deliverance gives me the courage to keep showing up boldly, even in hard places.

At this particular hospital where I was working at the time, there was no teamwork or sense of unity. There was just a heavy, tense environment in which people looked out for their own interests. I remember one night during my night shift when I was bathing a patient. The routine was always the same. I'd prep the patient and clean their front side, and then I'd need someone to help me turn the patient over, so I could clean their backside. The nurses' station was right outside the patient's room, so when I was ready, I poked my head out and saw about four nurses sitting at their computers, charting. I asked, *"Can anybody help hold this patient while I get them clean?"*

Silence. Nobody said a word. Nobody even looked up. They just sat there like they didn't hear me. I was one eye roll away from shouting, *"Now I know y'all hear me—sitting there acting like y'all deaf or something!"* Then the Holy Spirit whispered, *"Not today, daughter. Let Me handle it."* I stood there for a moment, then I went back into the room and shut the door. A couple of minutes later, someone finally came in to help, but it was like pulling teeth to get assistance. When help did come, it was dripping with bad attitudes—the *"I know everything, and you can't tell me nothing"* energy was strong in that place.

Praying My Way Through Spiritual Warfare at Work

When I tell you I had to pray every single chance I got working at that place, please believe me! I had to put on the full armor of God daily, rebuke the enemy in Jesus's name, and declare victory over my life. Every shift, I had to rely on God to increase my peace and patience because the tension in that hospital was unreal. Some nights, I felt like I was fighting just to keep my joy in an environment that seemed determined to steal it. It finally reached the point where I said, "My sanity is more important. I know my worth, and I know I have options." Sometimes, God places us in difficult environments to be the light. While I was there, I made it my mission to hold my head high. I helped others even when they wouldn't help me. I treated everyone with kindness. I did my job with excellence, not because they deserved it, but because it pleased God.

I want you to realize this—the kingdom of darkness is real, and its goal is to lead us straight to destruction (John 10:10, NLT). When we lose sight of God in our daily lives, we leave ourselves defenseless, allowing the enemy to creep into our emotions, thoughts, careers, and relationships. Before we know it, we feel empty, stuck, and lost, searching for fulfillment in places that will never satisfy us. Here's the good news. You don't have to stay bound. By preparing for spiritual warfare, seeking deliverance, renouncing negative words, and breaking strongholds, we can step into the true freedom that Christ has promised us. The enemy tries to keep us distracted or send diversions our way, but once we recognize his tactics, we can armor up, take back our authority, and live the life of victory God intended for us (Ephesians 6:13, NLT). It's time to wake up, take action, and fight back.

What Deliverance Looks Like in Action

Mary Magdalene didn't just walk away from her past; she was delivered from it. She made a choice to follow the One who freed her, and in doing so, became one of the most powerful examples of transformation in the Bible. That's what spiritual warfare looks like. It's not just about recognizing the battle but embracing the victory Jesus has already won on your behalf. You may not be possessed, but oppression can still creep in. Like Mary Magdalene, freedom is your portion, and deliverance is just the beginning. So, what does deliverance actually look like in your everyday life? Deliverance isn't always loud, dramatic, or performed before a church congregation. Sometimes, it's a quiet moment of surrender in your prayer closet. Sometimes, it's the decision to walk away from a toxic relationship, break a generational cycle, or cut ties with environments that feed your insecurity or anxiety.

Deliverance can look like:

+ Catching a lie from the enemy mid-thought and choosing not to agree with it. *"I'm not good enough"* turns into *"I am fearfully and wonderfully made."*

+ Breaking soul ties with someone you know God has told you to release. You stop romanticizing the past and start healing forward.

+ Deleting the playlist or unfollowing accounts that stir up lust, comparison, or rebellion. You guard your gates and protect your peace.

+ Choosing forgiveness even when the offense feels fresh. You let go not for them, but for your freedom.

+ Laying hands on yourself in prayer, renouncing negative words spoken over you, and declaring God's truth out loud. You no longer wait for someone else to free you. You walk in your God-given authority.

> ♥**Real Talk Moment:**
> You can't cast out what you secretly coddle. Freedom starts when you're done entertaining what's been oppressing you.

Deliverance is a daily decision to align yourself with truth, walk in obedience, and resist what once had a hold on you. It's choosing peace over people-pleasing, clarity over confusion, and freedom over fear. You don't have to wait for a church service or a deliverance minister to begin the process. You can partner with the Holy Spirit right where you are and invite Him into the broken, heavy, or hidden places. That's the beauty of God's presence; it's accessible, powerful, and personal. So if you're asking, *Lord, how do I break free?* Know that it starts with believing that you can, and then walking it out one obedient step at a time. Deliverance isn't a one-time event. It's a lifestyle of freedom.

Before you begin walking in deliverance, make sure you're truly ready to let go. Partial deliverance leaves the door cracked open. If this is your first time, seeking guidance from a trusted spiritual leader or deliverance minister is wise. Jesus warned in Matthew 12:43–45 (NLT) that when an unclean spirit leaves a person, it may return with seven more spirits even worse than before, if the house remains empty. That's why it's crucial to fill those newly vacated spaces with God's Word, consistent prayer, and the fruits of the Holy Spirit. Don't just get free, stay free.

Cultivated BOSS Method™ Tie-In: Obedient to God's Call

The second pillar of the Cultivated BOSS Method™ is Obedient to God's Call, because recognizing spiritual warfare is only the first step. The real change happens when you act on what God reveals. Obedience is when you leave the toxic relationship, renounce the soul tie, forgive the offense, or fast when God says fast. In those quiet acts of obedience, freedom becomes your lifestyle, not just a moment. God doesn't call you to fight alone but to follow Him into victory.

Your Daily Battle Plan for Breakthrough

Here are some strategies to help you equip yourself for deliverance and spiritual warfare.

1. Pray with Honesty and Humility. – Talk to God throughout your day—while driving, getting ready, or taking a break. Ask Him

to remove anything not aligned with His will, so you can move forward in peace.

2. **Forgive and Let Go.** – Unforgiveness keeps you stuck. Release bitterness in prayer, so you can walk in peace and focus on what God has for you.

3. **Identify the Root of Your Struggles.** – Take time to reflect on recurring issues like worry or fear. Ask God to reveal the root cause of the issue, so you can begin the healing process.

4. **Renounce and Break Agreement with the Enemy.** – When negative thoughts creep in, don't accept them. Speak against them in Jesus's name and replace them with God's word in the Bible.

5. **Put on the Armor of God Daily** – Take 30 seconds to pray: *Lord, I put on the full armor of God today—guard my mind, protect my heart, steady my steps, and help me stand strong in Your truth. In Jesus's name, Amen.*

6. **Renew Your Mind with the Word.** – Post Bible verses on sticky notes where you'll see them daily and meditate on them during stressful moments to keep your mind anchored in God's truth.

7. **Stay Rooted in the Body of Christ.** – Stay connected to faith-filled believers through church, mentorship, or community. You weren't meant to walk this journey alone.

8. **Walk in Your God-Given Authority.** – You have authority in Christ. Use it daily. Speak Scripture out loud over your life, pray with boldness, and shut down the enemy's lies the moment they show up. Remember, you're not fighting for victory. You're fighting from it.

9. **Stand firm in the victory Jesus has already won (Colossians 2:15, NLT).** – Declare God's promises over your life, and rebuke the enemy's lies daily (Luke 10:19, NLT).

Guarding Your Gates: The Power of What You Allow In

Growing up, I was obsessed with scary movies. The thrill, the suspense—I couldn't get enough. I had two grandmothers, Grandma Canary and Grandma Mary, both of whom have passed on. At different times in my life, would shake their heads and say, "That stuff invites the enemy in." I'd roll my eyes and think, *Grandma, everything isn't the devil—geesh!* Then I'd laugh to myself and think, *They're just old school.* Little did I know, they were absolutely right. I was unknowingly giving the enemy access to plant seeds of fear, anxiety, and negativity in my mind. The enemy isn't always loud and obvious. He's sneaky because he is looking for any opening to influence us, especially when we're most vulnerable. What better time than when we're entertaining fear, darkness, and destruction?

I remember watching a horror movie alone one night, convinced it was just harmless entertainment, but when I turned off the TV, I felt an overwhelming sense of fear and heaviness in my room. Every creak and every shadow suddenly felt alive. At one point, I was ready to rebuke the coat rack because it looked suspicious in the dark. I was uneasy, paranoid, and filled with fear, *but why?* What I had just exposed my eye and ear gates to was still lingering in my spirit. That's when I started realizing not everything is "just entertainment." Our eye and ear gates are the spiritual doors to our souls. What we see and hear enters our hearts and minds. If we constantly expose ourselves to things that glorify fear, lust, greed, or anger, those things start taking root in our spirit. The Bible warns us in Luke 11:34 (NLT): *"Your eye is like a lamp that provides light for your body. When your eye is healthy, your whole body is filled with light. But when it is unhealthy, your body is filled with darkness."*

This applies to more than just scary movies. As busy women, we're constantly consuming content, whether it's TV shows, music, social media, or conversations at work. Without realizing it, we allow certain influences to shape our mindsets, emotions, and spiritual atmosphere. *What kind of music are you feeding your spirit? What conversations are you constantly listening to? What shows are shaping your perspective on relationships, success, and self-worth?* Protecting our spiritual gates is not about legalism. It's about wisdom. (Legalism is a strict, rule-based approach to faith that focuses on religious laws rather than a relationship with God.) This isn't about making a list of dos and don'ts. It's about being mindful of what shapes your thoughts, emotions, and spiritual well-being. If something feeds fear, anxiety, comparison, or negativity, it's time to filter it out. I've learned to be more intentional about what I allow into my spirit because what I feed myself spiritually directly affects how I think, feel, and live. I'll say that both of my grandmothers were right. Now, I choose to guard my gates. *What about you?*

Jesus didn't just deliver her from torment; He restored her identity and gave her purpose. Luke 8:2 (NLT) tells us that Mary Magdalene had been afflicted by seven demons. She wasn't just dealing with physical pain; this was deep, spiritual oppression. When she encountered Jesus, everything changed. He cast the unclean spirits out of her, and instead of being defined by her past, she became a devoted follower of Christ. She was no longer bound; she was sent. Mary was among the first to witness the resurrection and boldly conveyed a risen Savior's message. That's the power of true deliverance. It doesn't just break chains, it rewrites your story.

Called to Stand Apart & Walk in Authority

Jesus prayed for us in John 17:15–16 (NLT): *"I'm not asking you to take them out of the world, but to keep them safe from the evil one. They do not belong to this world any more than I do."* We are set apart, but that doesn't mean we're exempt from spiritual battles. The Holy Spirit has given us power and authority to cast out unclean spirits, break free from negative emotions, and overcome destructive behaviors. Instead of avoiding these struggles, we should take them to God in prayer and ask Him for wisdom in areas we don't fully understand. Seeking guidance from trusted spiritual leaders can also bring clarity and support. Satan is after your soul. If we want to grow deeper in our walk with Christ, we can't conform to worldly values. Instead, we must live a life fully surrendered to God. True deliverance and spiritual warfare start within us; we must be prepared to fight. Take the next step in your journey. Visit www.eyfbook.com to download the "Self-Deliverance & Spiritual Warfare Prayers Guide" to help you break free from spiritual bondage and walk in authority. It's time to walk in freedom!

CHAPTER 5

MASTER SPIRITUAL DISCIPLINE AND MATURITY

"Discipline is the highest form of self-love. What you're not disciplined in, you don't really love."
(Thomas, n.d.)

Do You Have Oil in Your Lamp?

Let's start this chapter with a parable that hits deep—the story of the wise and foolish virgins from Matthew 25. Jesus tells the story of ten virgins who took their lamps and went out to meet the bridegroom. Five were wise and brought extra oil. Five were foolish and brought nothing. While the bridegroom delayed, they all fell asleep, but the cry rang out at midnight. "Here's the bridegroom! Come out to meet him!" The wise virgins were ready. Their lamps were still burning, but the foolish ones had to run off to buy more oil. By the time they returned, the door was shut. The bridegroom said something terrifying. "Truly I tell you, I don't know you." (Matthew 25:1–13, NIV)

Let that sit for a moment. These women looked the part. They were all dressed for the occasion. They had lamps. They were waiting just like everyone else, but only half of them were prepared for the moment that truly mattered. The oil in this story represents something deeper—spiritual readiness, intimacy with God, discipline, and maturity.

> **●Real Talk Moment:**
> Looking the part doesn't mean you're ready. God is checking for oil, not outfits.

Who exactly is the bridegroom in the Bible? It's Jesus. Yep, our Savior is often described as the Bridegroom, and guess who the bride is? Us. The Church. It is all of us who believe in Him. It's a beautiful image of His deep, faithful love for us. Just like a groom prepares for his wedding day, Jesus is preparing to return for a bride who's ready, spiritually mature, fully devoted, and ready to walk in intimacy with Him. He's not coming back for a lukewarm church; He's coming for one that's watching, waiting, and keeping her lamp full.

Let me ask you right here at the start. *Do you have oil in your lamp, or are you spiritually unprepared, coasting through your walk with God, and hoping you'll "get it together" later?* I've been there. I was once a foolish virgin. I had the look. I showed up at church. I knew how to say, "God is good," and I'd pray when it was convenient, but I had no oil. No consistency. No real discipline. I didn't understand that these spiritual practices weren't boxes to check. They were tools to keep my lamp burning for the long haul.

> **●Real Talk Moment:**
> Reading your Bible isn't a chore, it's spiritual survival.

When Discipline Meets Darkness: A Clinical Lesson in Spiritual Readiness

Let me take you back to my days in grad school while I was working on my master's degree. I had a clinical rotation that was almost an hour and a half away, and let me tell you, clinical hours are no joke. They're not optional. They're necessary for graduation, and they're how you get the hands-on experience you need to become a nurse practitioner or any other profession that requires them, so when I say I was desperate to find a preceptor, I mean it.

At one point, things had gotten so tight in my program that I thought I'd have to sit out for 12 weeks. That would've delayed my whole graduation plan, but God! He always has a ram in the bush. I was working on the floor as a registered nurse when I struck up a conversation with another nurse who had recently finished her family nurse practitioner degree. She gave me this providers contact info but warned me, "She's kind of...different. She prays for her patients and everything."

I remember thinking, *Uh, how is that weird? That sounds like a bonus.* At that point, I was thinking, *Look, I'll take a prayer and a prescription. Just get me a clinical site!* Little did I know that this woman wasn't praying to the God I served. When I first met this doctor, I remember sitting in her office and crying my eyes out. She had just told me that I was going to touch many lives through Christ, help a lot of people, and I'd travel all over the country doing so. I was moved and overwhelmed, and I honestly felt like God was confirming my purpose, but right there in the middle of my tears, she looked at me, smirked, and said, "Why do you keep crying like a White woman?" That was my first red flag.

I remember thinking, *Excuse me, ma'am... You just prophesied over my life. I think I have a right to shed a few tears, and what is crying like a White woman supposed to mean?* I brushed it off as an odd comment. She was from a different country; maybe it was just a cultural difference between us. Still, it didn't sit right. What I should've done at that moment was test the spirit behind her words. The Bible tells us in 1 John 4:1 not to believe every spirit but to test them to see whether they are from God. I should've paused, prayed silently, and asked the Holy Spirit for discernment before receiving anything spoken over my life because not every "prophetic" word comes from the throne of Heaven.

She spoke about other people doing voodoo, often casually, as if it were normal. Although she never outright said she practiced it herself, there was a spiritual heaviness about her clinic that I couldn't ignore. She sold crystals to patients "for specific uses," not décor. Now, don't get me wrong. There's nothing inherently wrong with having crystals. They can be pretty to look at, and they make great home decor, but as believers in Christ, when we start depending on objects like crystals to manifest healing, protection, or peace, we're essentially placing our faith in something other than God. It becomes a subtle form of idolatry—putting creation in the place of the Creator—and that's where the danger lies. There was a heavy spiritual atmosphere in that place, and I felt it. She could read people's lives and say things they hadn't told her, but it wasn't the Holy Spirit revealing that. It was something else. It made my spirit uneasy, like something just wasn't right. I could feel in my gut that it wasn't from God. I wanted to say, "Please don't let her lay hands on you. Run!"

> 💬**Real Talk Moment:**
> Accuracy doesn't always mean anointing. The devil knows details too.

Here's the thing. When you're pulling from demonic sources for spiritual power, you can still deliver accurate information. That's the deception. You may say something about someone's life that sounds prophetic, but if it didn't come from the Holy Spirit, it's not revelation. It's divination. It's spiritual theft, obtaining information illegally from the spirit realm, and Satan doesn't mind giving you accurate details if it means keeping people in bondage. He uses just enough truth to hook you, but the goal is always control, confusion, or counterfeit peace. It may look like healing, insight, or a breakthrough on the surface, but underneath, it opens doors to oppression, fear, dependency, and spiritual blindness.

When people are deeply involved in things of the kingdom of darkness, whether it's witchcraft, occult practices, or other demonic influences, they can attach curses, spells, or demonic assignments to everyday objects. These items can serve as open doors for spiritual oppression if we aren't careful. Which is exactly why I don't do mystery casseroles, random oils, or *gifts* from folks I don't know like that. I'm not about to let a demon hitch a ride in my purse, talking 'bout, *Thanks for the invitation.* Not today, Satan.

I didn't eat anything she gave me. I limited what I touched. One time, she used my pen and tried to give it back. I looked her in the eye and said, "You can keep it." That pen was officially retired, but I'll be honest, my spiritual confidence was low. I was juggling school, work, clinicals, and family. I wasn't consistently feeding myself with the Word of God. I wasn't spiritually built up. I was like a virgin with an empty lamp—still going through the motions, but not fully prepared.

Maybe if I had been spiritually stronger, I would've been led by the Holy Spirit to minister to her to help her turn around, but I wasn't thinking about the Kingdom. I was just trying to get through. I was not out here trying to be a junior prophet. I was just trying to survive my rotation and not bring anything unholy home with me.

Then came the dream. My older sister called and said, "I had a dream last night, and you need to hear it. Now, just to give you some context, she, along with my two younger sisters and a few other close family members, already knew about the doctor I had been shadowing. In the dream, she and I were running down a sidewalk, and muddy footprints were chasing us. We couldn't see what was behind us, but the trail was clear, and the footprints were right behind us." She ended up saying we made it home eventually, but I was acting weird, like whatever was chasing us had negatively come over me. After we talked the dream over, we prayed for protection, and we asked God to cancel anything that Satan was trying to devise against us.

The next day, I showed up at the clinic and sat in on our first patient. The doctor came in, chatting as usual. While she was talking with the patient, I glanced down, and I saw that she had boots on. Guess what was on her boots? MUD! This wasn't just a little backyard garden mud. These boots looked like she had stomped through a swamp right before coming into work. I remember thinking, *Why would she wear muddy boots like that to work?* Then, it hit me. My sister's dream. "The blood of JESUS!" I whispered under my breath. That dream was a warning, and God had highlighted who the warning was about. From that moment on, I took spiritual protection seriously. I prayed, quoted scripture in my head, and asked the Lord to guard me. That experience reminded me why oil matters. You can't wait until you're in the middle of a spiritual storm to fill your lamp. By then, it might be too late.

Let me be honest with you. During that season of my life, my schedule was swamped. Between working part-time as a nurse, attending grad school, driving nearly three hours round-trip for clinicals, and taking care of my family, I barely had time to breathe. I thought I was doing my best by simply surviving the day-to-day demands, but if I could go back and do it all over again, I would've made room for God first thing in the morning. I would have carved out space before the busyness began to pray, study, and fill my lamp with His oil because the truth is that when you don't make time to get spiritually filled, life will drain you.

Looking back, I realize how essential that discipline would've been—not just for protection, but for power, peace, and purpose. Spiritual maturity isn't about adding one more thing to your to-do list. It's about anchoring your day in the One who gives you strength to do it all.

What Jesus Modeled: A Life of Consistent Discipline

Mark 1:35 tells us that Jesus got up early while it was still dark and went to a quiet place to pray. That one verse alone speaks volumes about the spiritual discipline He practiced. Jesus prioritized His time with the Father before the demands of the day even began. It wasn't about convenience; it was about commitment. *Why?* Jesus knew what was coming. He knew His assignment. He was ready for the day before the day even started.

That is how spiritual discipline looks. It's not about being perfect; it's about being prepared. It's what separates the wise from the foolish. The wise woman gets up, even when she doesn't feel like it. The foolish one keeps saying, "I'll do it tomorrow," while her oil runs dry. Spiritual discipline is doing what your feelings don't feel like doing because your faith says it matters. It's choosing prayer over procrastination. It's choosing worship over worry. It's setting the alarm and getting up before your house wakes up, not because it's easy, but because you know the value of being filled before the noise of the day begins.

> **●Real Talk Moment:**
> If your discipline only shows up when it's convenient, it's not discipline, it's a mood.

Jesus didn't rely on human strength. He operated through the power of the Holy Spirit and modeled how that looks—consistent prayer, solitude, submission, and time in the Word. This wasn't just something Jesus did; it was who He was. If we're going to walk in power, discernment, and purpose, we've got to follow His example. Discipline isn't glamorous, but it's foundational. *Spiritual maturity?* That's what grows when we show up daily, even in the quiet.

Here's the truth. A spiritually mature woman doesn't just talk about God. She walks with Him daily. She opens the Bible when no one's watching. She confesses sin, submits her plans, checks her heart, and lives for an audience of One. She might mess up, but she gets back up because her foundation is discipline, and her fruit is maturity.

Cultivated BOSS Method™ Tie-In: Obedient to God's Call

Discipline isn't just about structure. It's about obedience. The second pillar of the Cultivated BOSS Method™ is Obedient to God's Call, because walking in spiritual maturity means doing what God says, even when it's inconvenient, unpopular, or uncomfortable. Obedience looks like waking up early to pray when your flesh says sleep. It looks like walking away from spiritual compromise, even when no one else sees it. It's not perfection God is after. It's participation in His plan. When you say yes to discipline, you're saying yes to transformation.

Keys to Keeping Your Lamp Full

Here are a few strategies to help you master self-discipline and maturity.

1. Meditate on Psalm 37:5 (NLT): *"Commit everything you do to the Lord. Trust him, and He will help you."* – Ask yourself, *In what area of my life have I not fully surrendered?*

2. Reflect on the reasons why you lack spiritual discipline and maturity. – (lack of understanding, difficulty connecting with God, lack of routine or procrastination, negative attitudes, and little motivation.)

3. Visualize the spiritually mature version of yourself. – Live a lifestyle of daily submission, prayer, fasting, worship, and service.

4. Write down your desired outcomes of having a mature relationship with God. – Set routine actions to take steps to reach your desired outcomes. – (when you will be praying, fasting, reading/studying the Bible, and memorizing and meditating on scripture.)

5. Capture negative thoughts and replace them with God's truth from Scripture. – Speak Biblical affirmations over your life daily.

6. Practice daily hospitality by being welcoming, humble, a good listener, and open to growth.

7. Spiritual maturity takes time. – Identify one area where you feel stuck or dissatisfied, and ask God how He wants to grow you there. Let that become your starting point for change. Spiritual maturity means not throwing a holy tantrum when God doesn't do what you want, when you want.

8. Model the example of Jesus in your life by prioritizing the needs of others before your own, being grateful for what you have, forgiving others, confessing your sins, submitting to His will and authority, and making time for solitude and reflection with God.

Spiritual Readiness is Eternal Readiness

"Then the King will say to those on his right, 'Come, you who are blessed by my Father; take your inheritance, the kingdom prepared for you since the creation of the world. For I was hungry and you gave me something to eat, I was thirsty and you gave me something to drink, I was a stranger and you invited me in, I needed clothes and you clothed me, I was sick and you looked after me, I was in prison and you came to visit me" (Matthew 25:34-36, NIV). Spiritual readiness isn't just about surviving the day. It's about being prepared to stand before the King. Every act of obedience, compassion, and faithfulness is preparation for eternity, where your readiness will be rewarded with a kingdom that's been waiting for you since the beginning of time.

We are in the waiting season, just like the virgins in the parable. The truth is that Jesus is the Bridegroom. He's coming to a church that's ready. *Will you be ready, or will you be off and "buying oil" when He arrives?* Let's choose to be wise women—women of preparation, obedience, and discipline, women who love God enough to show up for Him daily, and women with full lamps. One day, when the door opens, I want to hear Him say, "Well done, my good and faithful servant."

Believe me when I say that I get it. Your days are long. You're juggling career, family, and responsibilities, and you're probably running on empty most days, but you've got this because you've got God. If you lay down your own agenda daily and allow the Holy Spirit to take the lead, you will be amazed at how your capacity, peace, and spiritual strength will increase. God's grace is enough to help you balance it all, but it starts with discipline and surrender.

I want you to remember that one day, we all will be judged, and I'm sure we all want to hear those beautiful words, "Well done, my good and faithful servant," instead of the haunting words, "Depart from me, for I do not know you." These earthly bodies are temporary, and God gives us free will to decide how to use them. I thank God for giving us the Holy Spirit to help us be disciplined because without the Holy Spirit, we would not be able to accomplish this in our own strength.

> "Rejoice always, pray continually, give thanks in all circumstances; for this is God's will for you in Christ Jesus."
> — (1 Thessalonians 5:16–18, NIV)

The development of spiritual discipline and maturity doesn't happen overnight; it takes time, but it's worth it. What you do now determines whether your lamp is burning when the cry goes out. Visit www.eyfbook.com to download the "Spiritual Discipline Tracker: 21-Day Fruit-Bearing Habit Builder" to help you develop essential habits and master spiritual discipline and maturity.

CHAPTER 6

WALK BY THE FRUITS OF THE SPIRIT

> *"By their fruit you will recognize them. Do people pick grapes from thornbushes, or figs from thistles?"*
> **(Matthew 7:16, NIV)**

Mary and Martha: Choosing What Matters Most

Let's talk about two sisters in the Bible who give us a front-row seat to one of the biggest tension points in a woman's life—being busy versus being still. Mary and Martha were close friends of Jesus. Their home was a place He often visited. In Luke 10:38–42 (NIV), we see the two sisters respond very differently when Jesus comes over. Martha, the ultimate hostess and caretaker, immediately gets to work—cleaning, cooking, and making sure everything looks just right. I imagine her wiping down counters that were already clean and fluffing pillows no one was going to sit on because that's what we do when we want to look like we have it all together.

> 💬**Real Talk Moment:**
> How many times have you been breaking your neck to perform
> when Jesus was just asking for your presence?

Meanwhile, Mary chooses a different route. She sits herself right at Jesus' feet, soaking up His words. She is unbothered by the to-do list. Martha gets frustrated (who can blame her when you're feeling like you're doing all the work?) and basically asks Jesus, "Can you please tell my sister to help me?" Jesus lovingly corrects her by saying, *"Martha, Martha, you are worried and upset about many things, but few things are needed—or indeed only one. Mary has chosen what is better, and it will not be taken away from her"* (Luke 10:41–42, NIV). Can you imagine being in that moment? You are so busy, overwhelmed, and distracted, thinking you're doing what's most important, only to realize you've been missing the very thing your soul needs most? Pause for a second and picture yourself in Martha's shoes. *How often do you get caught up in the noise and neglect the peace that comes from simply sitting at Jesus's feet?*

This story isn't about whether chores are bad or serving is wrong. It's about what matters most in the moment. Mary chose intimacy with Jesus over activity for Jesus, and that's the heart of this chapter. Walking by the fruit of the Spirit means choosing to be led by God's character over our own impulses, busyness, or emotions.

Many of us are modern-day Marthas without realizing it, especially career women. We can get caught up in our roles, responsibilities, to-do lists, and expectations, all while missing the greater invitation to simply be in God's presence and allow the Holy Spirit to shape who we are.

When I Chose Distraction Over Devotion

Just like Mary, let me share a part of my journey that taught me how critical it is to stop striving and start abiding. I grew up in a huge Baptist church, where I was baptized at 11 years old. Growing up as a kid and young adult, I never understood the Fruits of the Spirit. I would hear my pastor talk about them, but for some reason, I didn't think they applied to me. Even after being baptized, I would still live life the way I wanted to live it. I felt like a tree split in two. One side bore good fruit, but I had another side that bore bad fruit. The truth was I was a single tree with some bad roots. Just like Martha, I was busy "doing" but had no idea how to be rooted in Christ and bear good fruit. I thought that going to church, showing up, and checking off boxes meant I was doing well spiritually, but my actions weren't always producing the fruit God wanted in me.

Understanding Our Spiritual Makeup

As human beings, we are tripartite, which means we are made up of three parts. We are made up of a spirit, a soul, and a body. The body, the breath of God (which produces life), and a person as a whole (their mind, consciousness, feelings, and desires) is a combination of the soul. Our human spirits are our true selves that go beyond the physical world. Our spirit is the innermost part of our being, meaning that it is located at the center of our existence or nature. We are able to communicate with the Holy Spirit that dwells within us through our spirits. The body is our physical senses, such as seeing, smelling, hearing, tasting, and touching. The Bible says that our bodies are a temple for the Holy Spirit, so the Holy Spirit dwells in our entire being.

The Bible describes the Holy Spirit as the third person of the Trinity—the Father, the Son, and the Holy Spirit. He is God Himself who consoles us, teaches, guides, and intercedes on our behalf. The Holy Spirit has feelings and intellect. He bears spiritual fruits and gifts. The Holy Spirit distributes gifts as He sees fit, such as faith, word of wisdom, word of knowledge, the ability to speak in tongues, the ability to interpret tongues, and the ability to heal, perform miracles, and prophesy. The Holy Spirit is the source of our strength.

When Busyness Becomes a Burden

It was difficult for me when I started my nursing career 12 years ago. I was trying to tackle it without fully relying on God. I was a lukewarm Christian, meaning I had one foot in and one foot out of the kingdom of God. The Bible tells us that a lukewarm Christian is worse than a non-believer. My prayer life was routine, and I was not eager to get into God's Word. I was living out my own will and not the will of God. Instead of standing out, I was blending in. This spilled over into my career. I would have anxiety and fear when I went to work because I lacked confidence in my knowledge, especially when I was a brand-new nurse.

It was a lot to take in. Now, it's human nature for us to have these emotions, especially when we're starting something new, but when we don't know how to turn those over to God and rely on the truth of Scripture, that's when it becomes a problem. I would have anxiety and fear about understanding the charting system, doing my patient assessments, managing medication passes, obtaining lab work, and whatever else came along with nursing because I was afraid of messing up. Anxiety and fear had such a hold on me that sometimes I felt like I couldn't even think clearly. I would go home and be on the verge of tears while rethinking my entire career choice. I would compare myself to others and think about how other nurses did their jobs better than I did. I'd look at some of those nurses like they had superhero capes under their scrubs, while I was barely holding it together, but little did I know, they more than likely had their own set of issues or insecurities. Plus, I carried the burden of wanting to please the other nurses around me, which weighed me down tremendously.

> **🗨Real Talk Moment:**
> Stop comparing your behind-the-scenes to someone else's
> highlight reel. We're all in process.

People-pleasing will drain you dry because you're constantly seeking validation from people who can never fill you the way God can. What truly matters is pleasing God, not earning the approval of others. One way to overcome people-pleasing is to start each day by asking God, "Lord, how can I serve You today?" instead of wondering what everyone else expects from you. When your focus shifts to honoring God first, you'll stop bending over backward trying to impress people who didn't die on the cross for you. It reminds me of how Martha was distracted and anxious about all the preparations, while Mary sat peacefully at Jesus's feet. I was doing the most, trying to look the part, sound the part, and stay busy like Martha, but inside, I was falling apart because I wasn't rooted in the right place.

> **🗨Real Talk Moment:**
> You can be doing all the right things and still be a spiritual
> wreck if you're disconnected from the Source.

The Shift: From Routine to Relationship

Now, let's fast-forward to midway through my nursing career. After gaining some experience and getting a little practice under my belt, I had developed confidence as a nurse, and I did my job well, but I was lacking a true relationship with God. I wasn't always operating in love by showing kindness and compassion to my coworkers and patients. Some days, my mindset automatically started negatively from just the thought of having to go to work. I would find myself thinking: *Here we go again. I have to go and spend 12 hours with these annoying coworkers and patients. I hope such and such isn't working tonight.* I also thought: *I really hope such and such is working tonight instead, so the night will go smoother.*

At the beginning of my career, I loved nursing, but only when it was convenient. I had no joy in what I was doing. I only had momentary, fluctuating happiness from time to time with my career when things were going well. Most days, I was clocking in with a grumble and clocking out doing the electric slide, forgetting I had prayed for the very job I was complaining about! It's funny how that works. We spend time begging God for a position or whatever we want in life, and when we finally get it, we complain about it or realize it's not what we wanted.

> **●Real Talk Moment:**
> Don't curse the blessing you once begged God for. Gratitude changes everything.

My patients and coworkers were able to steal my peace whenever they did or said something that would get under my skin. I would find myself frustrated and upset. I would rarely preach the Word of God in the workplace, so a lot of people didn't even know who I represented. I was timid when it came to discussing the Bible because I did not make the time to read it. The fruits of the Holy Spirit were not evident in my life during this time because I was operating in the flesh, allowing my body and emotions to lead. I was acting like Martha, busy and productive, but disconnected from the presence and peace of Jesus.

Bearing Good Fruit: My Transformation

Looking back on the other half of my nursing career, I felt a deep passion for it when I began to seek God out and allow Him to take the lead. I was able to see more clearly and align my heart's posture with the Word of God by confessing daily that my life was not my own and that I wanted the life of Christ. I realized I had to stop being a lukewarm Christian and fully rely on God and His Word. When I began to practice bettering my spiritual discipline and maturity in my personal life, the results began to overflow into my career.

At my previous job, I would preach the gospel openly and pray for my patients if they wanted prayer. I would have conversations with men and women about God and their daily struggles. Some of my patients would even say that I felt like their counselor. Many people often told me how my words were an encouragement, and appreciated me listening to them vent when they were going through something. I heard coworkers and patients say, "You should go into ministry; You are kind and understanding; You seem to get every-thing you ask for in life; Is your husband a pastor because you have a first lady demeanor?"

Even at my previous position prior to the last one, when I was working as a registered nurse, I would get comments like, "Girl, you have God's favor on you. Let me touch you a little bit, and may-be some of it will rub off on me." (LOL) The truth of the matter was that it wasn't my doing. I was walking in the fruits of the Spirit by allowing the Holy Spirit to lead my life. This caused me to bear good fruit, which showed through my actions. I was able to walk in love, joy, peace, patience, kindness, goodness, faithfulness, gentle-ness, and self-control through the power of the Holy Spirit. I also began making it a point not to complain before going into work. Whenever I caught myself getting ready to speak negatively or com-plain, I would stop and start thanking God instead for the job, the opportunity to serve, and the strength to get through the shift. That intentional practice began to soften my heart and shift my mindset.

Do you see the difference between how I started my nursing ca-reer to where I ended up? When I let go and let God, He was able to dig up dead roots of anxiety, fear, rejection, people-pleasing, and more. By the power of the Holy Spirit, I was able to become rooted in Christ.

No longer was I operating from a place of fear and anxiety. I learned how to combat that fear and anxiety by memorizing and meditating on Scripture. Whenever anxious thoughts would try to creep in, I would remind myself of God's promises and speak His Word over my life until peace took over. One of my favorite scriptures that I memorized was 2 Timothy 1:7. It says, *"For God has not given us a spirit of fear or timidity, but of power, love, and a sound mind"* (NKJV).

I was not letting my circumstances, patients, and coworkers determine if I was going to have a good day or not. I had already decided at the start of my day that it was going to be a good one, regardless of what I was facing. I was not out to please people but to please God. John 15:4 says, *"Remain in me, as I also remain in you. No branch can bear fruit by itself; it must remain in the vine. Neither can you bear fruit unless you remain in me"* (NIV). This means we can only produce good fruit when we stay connected to Jesus. The Bible says that Jesus is the way, the truth, and the life.

If Jesus is the vine, and we are the branches connected to Him, we will bear good fruit. John 15:6 says, *"If you do not remain in me, you are like a branch that is thrown away and withers; such branches are picked up, thrown into the fire, and burned"* (NIV). This means that without Him, we have nothing, and it leaves a doorway open for Satan to come in. When we love God and follow His commandments, it brings forth the fruits of the Holy Spirit.

We must all do occasional fruit checks to see what sort of fruit we are bearing in our lives. The evidence will show when we stay connected to the kingdom of God. We will naturally bear good fruit, but when we are disconnected and operating under the influence of the kingdom of darkness, bad fruit will start to show up in our lives. The Bible says you will know a tree by the fruit it bears. Think about it this way. When we allow hate to take root in our hearts, that's a seed from the kingdom of darkness, and it produces bad fruit, but when we choose to love, even when it's hard, that's evidence of the kingdom of God at work in us. Fear is another seed from the kingdom of darkness, but when we walk in peace, we are showing the world that God is the One leading our lives.

Don't be discouraged if you have some roots in the wrong places. God's grace allows room for healing and renewal to take place if we struggle with unpleasant emotions or sin. This is where we need to call on the Lord, confess our sins, repent, and ask for forgiveness. Seek out deliverance and be intentional about committing our lives to God. Eventually, I knew I had to seek God out to transform me from within by uprooting and removing things that were not of Him. According to the Bible, a good tree can neither bear bad fruit nor can a bad tree bear good fruit.

Just like Mary chose to sit and receive, rather than be consumed by what everyone else was doing, we too must choose what matters most—abiding in Christ. When we stay at His feet, we begin to bear the kind of fruit that reflects Him.

Cultivated BOSS Method™ Tie-In: Obedient to God's Call

The second pillar of the Cultivated BOSS Method™ is Obedient to God's Call, because fruit doesn't grow where there's disobedience. You can't bear spiritual fruit without spiritual surrender. When you choose to obey, even when it's uncomfortable, even when it costs your pride or plans, you create space for the Holy Spirit to lead. Obedience is where transformation begins. Mary didn't just choose intimacy, she chose obedience by sitting when the world said she should be doing. And when you do the same, the fruit will follow.

Strategies for Cultivating the Fruit of the Spirit

1. Self-Check Your Fruit. – Think about your life and whether you are producing good or bad fruit. Ask yourself, *Are my actions and behavior towards people and things good or bad?*

2. Replace the Rotten with the Ripe. – Write down all negative behaviors and then ponder on the nine fruits of the Holy Spirit (Galatians 5:22–23). For every negative behavior, put a line through it and replace it with a corresponding fruit.

3. Trust God to Lead Your Growth. – Have faith and rely on God to lead your life.

4. Make Fruitfulness a Lifestyle. – Use the fruits daily at home, at work, and while running errands. Set daily goals for how you plan to bear good fruit in real situations.

5. Pray for Purity and Power. – Pray and ask God to help cleanse and purify your heart and ignite the fruits of the Holy Spirit within you daily.

6. Extend Grace to Yourself. – Be patient with yourself and allow God's grace to help you through. Growth is a journey, not a sprint.

A Transformational Reminder for You

I want you to remember that true followers of Christ will be known by the fruit they bear. Daily repentance and reinforcement are necessary when bearing the fruits of the Spirit. If you're having a hard time hearing from God, check your fruit! Modeling the fruits of the Holy Spirit will be a lifelong process because we're constantly growing and going through different phases of our lives. God will refine these gifts as we continue to grow closer to Him. Just like Mary chose what was better, we must continue choosing time with Jesus over distractions, offense, and fleshly reactions.

Picture yourself right now. *Are you living like Martha—rushing around, overwhelmed, and anxious? Are you living like Mary—still, present, and listening to the voice of Jesus?* You'll gain more than peace when you intentionally shift from Martha mode to Mary mode. You'll gain clarity, wisdom, confidence, and the ability to bear fruit that lasts. You'll stop surviving and start thriving. The fruits of the Spirit will not only transform your personal life but also overflow into your career, relationships, and purpose. Visit www.eyfbook. com to download the "Fruit of the Spirit Bubble Map" to help you live out each fruit of the Spirit with purpose and joy.

> **🍎Real Talk Moment:**
> You're not too busy for Jesus, you're too distracted. Flip the script. Your breakthrough is at His feet.

CHAPTER 7

TIME MANAGEMENT AND ELIMINATING DISTRACTIONS

> *"Seek the Kingdom of God above all else, and live righteously, and*
> *he will give you everything you need."*
> **(Matthew 6:33, NLT)**

The Courage of Jael: A Woman Who Seized the Moment

Before we dive into my personal story, I want to introduce you to a woman in the Bible who is often overlooked but is a bold example of what it looks like to seize the moment and eliminate distractions—Jael.

Jael's story is found in Judges 4. She wasn't a warrior, prophetess, or queen. She was a homemaker, a wife living in a tent, who likely spent her days managing her household and going about her routine. However, when an opportunity presented itself for her to act on God's behalf, she didn't hesitate. She eliminated every distraction and fear in that moment, stepped into the assignment, and ultimately defeated Sisera, the commander of King Jabin's army. *How?* She invited him into her tent when he was fleeing for his life and gave him a place to rest, and once he fell asleep, she quietly took a tent peg and drove it through his temple, ending the battle in a way no one saw coming. She did this because Sisera was an enemy of Israel, oppressing God's people for years, and God had already declared through the prophetess Deborah that Sisera would be delivered into the hands of a woman. Jael's act was the fulfillment of that prophecy. With wisdom, discernment, and Divine timing, Jael showed us that victory doesn't always come on a battlefield. Sometimes, it happens in the quiet, unnoticed moments of obedience.

The Weight of Expectations and Busyness

Life will always be full of distractions and endless tasks. If we aren't careful, we will fill our days with things that feel essential but leave little to no room for God. It is up to us to release the unnecessary, surrender what we think is crucial, and prioritize our time with God, allowing everything else to fall into place. This reminds me of a season in my life that felt like pure chaos.

As I walked to my car, holding back tears, I picked up my phone to call my fiancé (at the time). He answered excitedly, but his tone changed when he heard the hurt and disappointment in my voice. As I held a sheet of paper with my picture on it, I read the words that crushed me. "A preliminary analysis of your responses indicates that you have FAILED the Family Nurse Practitioner National Certification Examination." I had just failed boards, and let me tell you, the word "FAILED" was in bold, capital letters as if the font itself was screaming at me like, "Girl, sit down somewhere."

I didn't have time to sit and dwell on my sorrows because I was getting married in a few weeks. As a single mom of a two-year-old, I had met the love of my life. At the time, we both were in the process of starting school. I was returning to school to receive my master's degree as a family nurse practitioner, and he was returning to receive his second bachelor's degree. This time, his degree would be in nursing. We were both in school full-time with clinical rotations, and we both were working part-time. Halfway through school, we had our first child together.

To add the icing on the cake, we decided to get married the same year we were both due to graduate. That meant we had to think about schoolwork, clinicals, working part-time, family life, and wedding planning—all happening at once. We would've been it if exhaustion and being overwhelmed had a face! I'm pretty sure if there were a reality show for "Most Overwhelmed Couple of the Year," we would've won. Hands down. No competition. We needed stability, peace, and rest, but I didn't know how to make space for it at the time.

Learning to Set Boundaries and Surrender

Feeling like everything was about to crumble, I had to devise a game plan. I leaned heavily on strict schedules to get us through school. I had to have a schedule for work, clinicals, sleeping, studying, and any little spare time was dedicated to wedding planning. I had all of the times mapped out as best as I could.

After getting married, I took a few months to buckle down and focus on studying because I did not want to fail boards again. Test day eventually came around, and my hard work paid off—I passed.

I tell this story to paint a picture of how easy it is to overpack our lives with demands and distractions. I developed strong organizational skills and discipline, and learned when to take mental breaks. I knew how to vocalize when I wasn't okay. I de-stress by walking, journaling, praying, and carving out time for connection with my family and friends. However, looking back, I now realize there could have been an easier way. I was doing all of this in my own strength. This is why Jael's story hits home for me. She wasn't striving to do everything. She wasn't trying to balance it all or prove her worth. She simply recognized the moment God gave her and moved in obedience. She wasn't distracted by fear, expectations, or her own limitations.

Recognizing the Distractions We Create

Looking back, I now see how I unintentionally put those demands on myself. We do it without realizing it. We pile on responsibilities, commitments, and expectations until we can't hear God over the noise. That season taught me to eliminate distractions, and now, I take intentional steps to avoid overloading my schedule with things that are unnecessary. As women, we have many tasks on our plates each day. When I used to work full-time as a nurse practitioner, I was stuck in a cycle of busyness. I got out of it by first realizing something was wrong with my routine. God was not a priority in my life.

> **🗨Real Talk Moment:**
> If you're too busy for God, you're doing more than He asked you to do.

The Shift: From Busyness to Balance

Previously, I discussed my busy routine and life with work and family life, but "What caused me to shift into managing my time and eliminating distractions?" Throughout my busy life, I've always felt this sense that I should be doing more or that there was more to life, but I just didn't understand it at the time. This was the Holy Spirit speaking to me, and I completely ignored Him. I mean, I tried to seek out the answers in worldly ways, such as moving around to different hospitals to work, advancing my career, and thinking a vacation would solve all of my problems. Lol, I wanted to take a vacation for everything. I was out here thinking a trip to the beach was going to fix my soul. I used to think, *Jesus, I just need some warm weather and a piña colada, then I'll be whole again.* Here is a spoiler alert. The sand didn't save me.

> **🗨Real Talk Moment:**
> The ocean is nice, but can't wash away what only Jesus can heal.

The problem was I would get away, but I would not seek God out. My deep connection with Him was not there, whether I was in my home state or on vacation. I had to learn the hard way. Once I finished my master's degree, I discovered that I was still getting this nudge that something was missing. I couldn't believe it. I thought to myself, *Here I am working in the desired career, and I still have this sense of not being fulfilled. What am I missing?* I wanted more for myself. I was tired of not living a life that wasn't fulfilled. When I took this to God in prayer, He started to reveal things to me over time, and I started paying attention to the quality of my walk with Him.

Just like Jael, I realized that I didn't need a title, a platform, or some big external achievement to make an impact. I needed to recognize the moment God was presenting me with and have the courage to respond. Unlike Jael, I was so distracted by the noise in my life that I couldn't see what God had placed right in front of me.

The Danger of Misplaced Identity

I wasn't seeing myself based on who God said I was as a woman of God. I sought validation from others and material things. Instead of going to God with a pure heart, I would pick and choose what situations I wanted to handle on my own and decide what situations I wanted God to deal with. I should have let Him be in total control of it all. I read the Bible from time to time, but it wasn't on a consistent basis. I allowed my family to be a distraction. When I set time aside to read the Bible or pray, I would easily brush that time to the side if my husband or kids came around, or if I received a phone call, or was pulled into one of the vast amounts of apps on my phone. My career was a distraction because I spent more time seeking ways to advance it than sitting with God.

I didn't see my identity as being rooted in Christ. It was rooted in my family and career. These all consumed my time because I did not set boundaries. When we don't set boundaries with the things of this world, they become idols. Idols can be anything we prioritize our time with before God. We can idolize anything, such as ourselves, food, hobbies, money, power, and relationships, and the list goes on. Any and everything that you put in God's place as the most important thing in your life is an idol.

Even comfort and sleep were idols for me. Most days, I would rather sleep in and be comfortable in my bed on a Sunday morning than get up and go to church. My bed was basically a spiritual stronghold.

It was like, "Sis, you don't need church. You need five more minutes." Five minutes would turn into fifty. However, like Jael, I had to learn that when God is calling you to act, you can't stay in your comfort zone. Jael didn't sit back and wait for someone else to take care of the battle. She didn't let fear, routines, or distractions keep her from stepping into the assignment God placed in front of her.

The Call to Intentional Living

God did not intend for us to be isolated. The church was created for God and His people to create a community where we can fellowship, share the gospel, grow, and learn as the body of Christ. We have to be intentional about our time spent with God. Nothing should be prioritized over the Lord. We have to tell others and ourselves sometimes. We need to say to ourselves, *Okay, from this time to this time I'm reading my Bible, praying or meditating on the word, or just sitting with God and reflecting on how good He has been.* Have it already made up your mind in advance, so you and others around you know that you cannot be distracted. When Sunday mornings come, already have it made up your mind that you're going to church. Get your clothes ready the night before and prep, so it's easier for you to get out the door in the mornings. Our mindsets have to be shifted.

Life is short, and if you don't believe me, just think about how long people lived in the Bible. Some were 900 years plus when they died. I want you to imagine something. Imagine God placing something on your heart for you to do, but you keep pushing it to the side for a later time; you keep procrastinating. One day, when you were in the middle of what procrastination looks like for you, whether that's sleeping in or watching your favorite movie or TV show, you heard a loud cry of command, the voice of an archangel, and the sound of the trumpet of God's return. *How would you feel?*

Would God say that He knows you, and you have been an obedient follower of Jesus Christ? Would you wish you had more time? I know I would feel like I needed more time, especially since I'm in a place right now, discovering all that God has for me. The truth is that when God says our time is up, our time is up. We need to take advantage of our time while we have it.

Your Jael Moment

When we start prioritizing God in our busy lives, He helps us see things more clearly. You start to see that the time you make for Him is essential, and you crave it more and more. Things you once stressed about become absolute. He begins to shift you to where He wants you to be. Without all of the distractions, you can hear from Him and be in tune when He begins to speak. You'll be aware of what your next move should be, and you will know if He is calling you into a new season.

Jael's obedience didn't just bring victory to her; it brought peace to an entire nation. That's the power of seizing the moment God puts before you, and I believe the same is true for you and me. The little moments we overlook because we're "too busy" may actually be the exact assignments God has prepared for us to shift generations. You may not feel like you're in a position of power. You may think you're "just a wife," "just a mom," "just an employee," or "just a student," but God has Divine moments waiting for you right in the middle of your routine, just like He did for Jael.

Your Jael moment might not involve fighting a Canaanite commander, but it may involve fighting the urge to binge an entire Netflix series when God's been nudging you to binge His Word instead. He might be asking you to hammer down that Amazon cart, break that phone addiction, or reevaluate your calendar that has more chaos than a calling. Your moment may be as simple as choosing prayer over procrastination, quiet time over chaos, or surrender over striving.

> **Real Talk Moment:**
> Netflix won't fulfill your purpose. Neither will your Amazon cart.

You were not created to live distracted, depleted, and disconnected from your Divine purpose. You were created to be bold in faith, obedient to God's call, and Spirit-led in every area of your life, but that requires you to pay attention, slow down, clear out the clutter, and make room for what really matters. I want to leave you with this truth. Victory happens in the quiet moments of obedience. Peace follows when you eliminate distractions and prioritize God. The life you desire—the fulfillment, the clarity, and the joy—it's waiting for you on the other side of intentional, Spirit-led choices. You don't need to do more. You need to do what matters. Your Jael moment is waiting. The question is, "Will you seize it?"

Cultivated BOSS Method™ Tie-In: Spirit-led

This chapter reveals what it really means to be Spirit-led, the third pillar of the Cultivated BOSS Method™. Being Spirit-led means you don't just fill your calendar, you follow God's cues. It means slowing down enough to hear the whisper of the Holy Spirit, even when everything around you is screaming for your attention. When Jael stepped into her moment, she wasn't reacting; she was responding to a Divine prompting. God is still prompting His daughters today. *Are you quiet enough to hear Him?* Let the Holy Spirit become your planner, peace, and daily strategist. You don't need more time. You need more alignment.

Practical Steps to Master Your Time & Minimize Distractions

Here are some strategies to help you manage your time better and eliminate distractions:

1. Identify Your Distractions. – Set aside 10 quiet minutes to list everything that distracts you, both obvious and hidden (like scrolling on social media, overthinking, or people-pleasing). Then, pray and ask God to reveal any distractions you don't even see and give you the strength to release them.

2. Prioritize & Plan with God. – Each Sunday or at the start of your week, sit with God and ask: *What should I focus on this week?* Write down 1–3 clear priorities and block out specific times for prayer, Bible reading, or quiet reflection on your calendar.

3. Pray for Peace & Clarity. – When you feel overwhelmed, pause and pray, *God, help me quiet the noise around and within me. Show me if I'm in the right season or if you're shifting me.* Take 5 minutes to sit in silence after you pray and listen for His guidance.

4. Practice full surrender by speaking this out loud every morning: *God, I give You control of my life today. I lay down my plans and choose Yours.*

5. Release your burdens onto God. – Set aside 5–10 minutes daily to talk to God about what's weighing on you—no filters, just honesty.

6. Read one scripture about His power and let it remind you that you're not carrying it alone. If the weight feels too heavy, reach out to a trusted spiritual leader for prayer.

7. If you don't already, start reading the Bible daily for 5-10 minutes. – A lot of us dread this because we don't understand the Bible, but it's ESSENTIAL in helping us get aligned with God.

8. Start your day asking yourself: *How can I honor God first today?* – Let that question shape your priorities and remind you that your goal is eternity, not perfection.

You're Being Cultivated: Living Each Day Through God's Greater Plan

Remember that our lives are short, and we don't know when our time will be up. We must seize the moment and take advantage of every God-given opportunity while on Earth. Ephesians 5:15–16 NLT says, *"...so be careful how you live. Do not live like fools, but like those who are wise. Make the most of every opportunity in these evil days."* There is a time and a season for everything. It's up to us to take advantage of our time by living out the life that God desires for us, so we are pleasing in the Lord's sight and ready when he returns.

You belong to the God who wants you to find rest, not just physical rest, but soul rest. He's not asking you to carry every burden or hustle your way to worthiness. He's inviting you to breathe, pause, and let Him lead you beside those quiet waters.

> **●Real Talk Moment:**
> You're not a robot, and even Jesus took naps on boats. Rest isn't weakness; it's wisdom.

Right now, before you jump back into your day, take a couple of deep breaths. Talk to God about what's on your mind. Lay down the to-do list, the stress, the overwhelm, and invite Him in. When you feel like your efforts aren't enough or when you feel behind, distracted, or defeated, remember this text. *"Therefore, my dear brothers and sisters, stand firm. Let nothing move you. Always give yourselves fully to the work of the Lord, because you know that your labor in the Lord is not in vain."*— (1 Corinthians 15:58 NIV)

Everything you do for God matters—even the quiet, behind-the-scenes obedience and the small steps to eliminate distractions and draw closer to Him. He sees it all, and He honors it. You're not behind. You're not forgotten. You're being cultivated. Your Jael moment is waiting, and when you seize it, you'll begin to see your life, your time, and even your struggles in a brand-new light—through the lens of God's greater plan. Visit www.eyfbook.com to download the "Distraction Detox Plan" to recenter your mind on God and eliminate what's keeping you from divine focus and peace.

CHAPTER 8

ENGAGE IN EFFECTIVE PRAYER AND MEDITATION

> *"But when you pray, go away by yourself, shut the door behind you, and pray to your Father in private. Then your Father, who sees everything, will reward you."*
> **(Matthew 6:6 NLT)**

The Power of a Praying Woman: Hannah's Story

Before I share my personal prayer journey, let's talk about a woman who truly knew the power of heartfelt prayer—Hannah. Hannah's story, found in 1 Samuel Chapter 1, is one that every woman can relate to on some level. She was a woman who carried deep sorrow, longing, and disappointment. Year after year, she went to the temple with her husband, Elkanah, while silently wrestling with the reality that she couldn't have children. To make matters worse, she was taunted by Elkanah's other wife, Peninnah, who had many children and never missed a chance to remind Hannah of what she lacked (1 Samuel 1:1-7, NIV).

Hannah's story isn't just about barrenness—it's about carrying a heavy weight in secret. It's about unfulfilled desires and wanting something so badly, but watching it slip through your fingers year after year. What changed everything for Hannah was how she handled that pain. One day, she went to the temple and poured her heart out before God. No routine prayers. No superficial words. It was raw, unfiltered, and desperate. She prayed so fervently that the priest thought she was drunk. She wasn't. She was surrendering everything she had left.

That's where the shift happened. God heard her prayer. He blessed her with a son, Samuel, and her private pain turned into a public testimony. Hannah's story taught me that effective prayer isn't about fancy words or religious routines. It's about honest surrender and a heartfelt connection with God.

My Prayer Journey: From Routine to Relationship

I wish I could say I always understood how true prayer looked, but that wasn't my story. "What is prayer?" I didn't always understand the power of prayer until I began to deepen my spiritual walk with God. I used to pray out of religious obligation because that's what we were "supposed" to do as Christians, but I didn't fully understand it. Prayer is how we communicate with God; after we pray, we should sit and listen for His response. However, like many of us, I had the prayer part down pat, but I never paused long enough to listen. I remember a season of my life when my prayers sounded like a broken record—day in and day out, the same old routine. I would thank Him for the day, ask Him to forgive me, and pray for my family's safety. I would throw in a quick request for a job opportunity or better finances. It was basically the Christian version of a pre-programmed voicemail. "Hey God, it's me again. Same requests. Talk soon. Amen."

> 💬**Real Talk Moment:**
> Stop leaving messages if your prayer life sounds like a broken voicemail. He's waiting for a real conversation.

The first major problem was that I was praying out of routine. My prayers weren't coming from my heart. It's like the same old song on repeat. I prayed out of habit instead of from the heart. My prayer life had no growth, so my intimate relationship with God was non-existent. As a matter of fact, it didn't even occur to me that I could have a deeper relationship with God at the time. Honestly, I think that's where so many of us go wrong. We assume that the "deep" things of God are reserved for other people—pastors, preachers, super spiritual folks but not us. We feel like God's got some kind of VIP list, and we're just hoping to sneak in on the guest pass.

The enemy wants you to believe that you can't connect with God or that your prayers aren't being heard. The truth is that God hears every prayer. Sometimes, He's just waiting for us to position our hearts to truly receive and surrender.

> 💬**Real Talk Moment:**
> Just because you've been saved for years doesn't mean you've been surrendered. God wants more than recited prayers on repeat.

A Time I Learned to Pray from the Heart

Before I met my husband, I had an experience that forced me to really learn how to pray differently. I became a single mom in a way that I never saw coming. It was during a time when my life felt like a complete whirlwind. I was trying to hold it together, but everything around me was falling apart. I met a guy who, at the time, seemed charming and sweet. Things moved quickly between us, and before I knew it, I found out I was pregnant before we even made it a whole year. The news shook me to my core. It wasn't a joyful, planned moment. Our relationship was already rocky and on the fence, and this pregnancy felt like it would somehow force us to "figure it out."

Ironically, before I got into this situation, I used to look at other women who had children outside of marriage, and I would quietly wonder why things seemed so hard for them. *Why was there so much chaos, arguing, and back-and-forth between them and their child's father?* I thought to myself, *Surely, people can co-parent without all the drama.*

Lo and behold, I ended up living that very story. Despite the growing tension, I tried to make things work with him, but there were constant disagreements. There were so many things we couldn't see eye to eye on. I remember one night vividly. I was at his mother's place, and we were discussing something. It escalated into a heated argument. At that moment, something clicked in me. I was only a couple of months pregnant, but I knew deep down that I was done. I thought to myself: *Just because I'm pregnant doesn't mean I have to stay in this toxic relationship. I can do better. I will do better for myself and my child.*

Even something as simple as deciding whose last name our daughter would have became a battle. We couldn't agree on anything. It was messy, and our daughter hadn't even been born yet. Fast forward to the day I gave birth. He was able to make it to the hospital to see her the day she was born, but the next day, when it came time to sign the birth certificate, he didn't make it. He had gotten into trouble and couldn't get there in time. In that moment, I took it as a clear sign from God. I made the decision to give her my last name and stand firm in moving forward without him.

What followed was a series of broken promises and letdowns. We would set up times for him to visit, and often he'd cancel at the last minute or have some excuse—car trouble or something came up. It was always something. It got to the point where I could've made a bingo card of his excuses—car trouble, something came up, missed the bus, my dog ate my keys... I tried to give him the benefit of the doubt, but eventually, I saw the pattern.

●Real Talk Moment:
If you can guess their excuse before they speak, it might be time to stop hoping for consistency and start praying for closure.

I remember having a hard but necessary conversation with him. I told him, "You're either going to be here for her or not." He said he wanted to, but his actions said otherwise. There came a point when I was done playing games, done with the back and forth, and done allowing partial commitment. I changed my number and made peace with the fact that he knew where to find us if he ever wanted to make an honest effort.

I won't pretend I handled everything perfectly. I was young, hurt, and disappointed, trying to do the best I could with what I had. I felt judged at times, both by others and myself, but I always tried to keep my daughter's best interests at heart.

To this day, I'm not sure where he is. He hasn't seen her since she was maybe one or two years old. I prayed many prayers during that season—for forgiveness where I was at fault, for healing over the things I couldn't change, and for wisdom on how to navigate it all.

One of my deepest prayers is for the day when I have the conversation with my daughter about everything—where she comes from, what choices I made, and how God was working even in the middle of our mess. I pray that God will guide that conversation, soften her heart, and help her understand that none of this defines her. I pray she will see how God has covered her, how her stepdad has stepped in and loved her like his own, and how God has used our story to bring beauty from brokenness.

Neoki is 10 now, but if her biological father ever showed up today, I would apologize to him and his family about how things turned out. I wouldn't stand in the way if he truly wanted to be a part of her life. My prayer is simply that God's will be done. I would tell him, "I forgive you and pray that God's will—not mine—be done." At the end of the day, this isn't about me. It's about the healing, restoration, and a future God wants to write, not the one I tried to force.

Take a moment and ask yourself: *What is one area of my life where I silently wish things had turned out differently?* Maybe it's a relationship, a career decision, or a season that left you feeling broken or disappointed. I want you to sit with that thought, but not from a place of regret. Instead, I want you to look at it through the lens of faith. The same God who turned Hannah's sorrow into joy and worked in my mess to create something meaningful is the same God who can turn that situation around for you.

The key is learning how to take that desire and that disappointment and bring it to God in intentional prayer, believing that even if you can't see it yet, He's already working behind the scenes. Your waiting is not wasted. God specializes in rewriting stories and making beauty out of broken places, but it starts when you release it to Him and pray with expectation.

How God Wants Us to Pray and Meditate

Matthew 6:5-8 teaches us that we shouldn't pray to impress others or use empty words. Instead, when we pray, we should go away by ourselves, shut the door, and pray to our Father in private. He will reward us. Jesus even gave us a template. He said, *"Our Father who art in heaven, Hallowed be thy name. Thy kingdom come. Thy will be done on earth, as it is in heaven. Give us this day our daily bread. And forgive us our trespasses, as we forgive those who trespass against us. And lead us not into temptation, but deliver us from evil: For thine is the kingdom, and the power, and the glory, forever. Amen"*—(Matthew 6:9-13 KJV). I had read and recited "The Lord's Prayer" for years without really internalizing it.

> **●Real Talk Moment:**
> God's Word isn't a casual read, it's a survival guide. Don't skim it, study it.

I knew the words but never really stopped to think about what I was agreeing to, but as I began to learn what it meant, it changed everything.

- "Our Father who art in Heaven" — I began to see Him as my loving Father.

- "Hallowed be thy name" — I learned how to honor and reverence Him.

- "Thy kingdom come. Thy will be done." — I stopped praying for my plans and started asking for His.

- "Give us this day our daily bread." — I trusted Him to sustain me and my daughter, even in the hardest seasons.

- "Forgive us...as we forgive others." — I asked God to help me forgive her father, myself, and anyone who had judged me.

- "Lead us not into temptation." — I prayed for wisdom, strength, and discernment.

- "For thine is the kingdom..." — I surrendered control.

Here's what I want you to know. Prayer isn't complete without meditation. Too often, as career women, we think prayer is just us doing all the talking, making all the requests, and checking off our spiritual to-do list before we move on to the next thing, but meditation is the other side of that coin. Meditation is how we slow down and give God room to speak back.

What Meditation Really Means

When I talk about meditation, I'm not talking about sitting cross-legged, humming "ommm." Christian meditation isn't about emptying your mind like the world teaches. It's about filling your mind with God's truth. Unlike regular meditation that focuses on self-awareness or mindfulness, Biblical meditation focuses on God, His Word, and the process of allowing His truth to shape your thoughts, heart, and life. Biblical meditation is intentional, purposeful reflection on God's Word and His presence. It's about chewing on scripture, letting it roll around in your heart and mind until it starts to shape the way you think, feel, and live. For a woman like you—a woman who's busy, ambitious, and always on the go—meditation isn't about adding another thing to your to-do list. It's about learning how to build sacred pauses into your life.

Here's how it looks in my life now. These days, I intentionally find small pockets of time throughout my day to call on God, thank Him, or simply acknowledge His presence. It could be while I'm driving to work, folding laundry, standing in line at the grocery store, or even going in between back-to-back meetings. Sometimes, I'll whisper, "God, I see You. Thank You for being here." Other times, I'll pause for a moment and say, "Lord, what are You trying to show me right now?" It doesn't have to be an hour-long session on your knees, although there's nothing wrong with that. It's the consistency and intentionality that matter.

How to Hear God's Voice in a Noisy World

Let's clear something up real quick: God is not silent. He speaks every day. *The problem?* We've turned up the volume on everything else. In the Bible, God spoke through burning bushes, dreams, angels, and even donkeys. He guided people through signs, visitations, and the teachings of Jesus Himself. He speaks through the Holy Spirit, and yes, He's still speaking. The question is, are you still enough to hear Him? Let's be real: if you're always distracted, you won't discern the difference between God's whisper and the world's noise. To hear from God clearly, you've got to create space for stillness. Silence isn't just peaceful, it's powerful. It tunes your spirit and clears the static of the world. That's where the whispers of Heaven break through.

It's not that God stopped speaking; you just might be trying to hear Him over your morning meeting, the household chaos, three client emails, a half-watched webinar, and that never-ending to-do list staring at you from the corner of your screen.

> **🗨Real Talk Moment:**
> If you keep asking God for direction but refuse to slow down long enough to listen, you're not waiting, you're just wandering in circles. Sometimes we need a holy pause before we get divine clarity.

The more intentional you are about sitting with God, through prayer, fasting, journaling, or just meditating on His Word, the more familiar His voice becomes. Like how Elijah didn't hear God in the earthquake or fire, but in the still, small voice (1 Kings 19:12). Sometimes His voice is a nudge. Other times, it's a verse that grabs your attention, and often, it's a peace that doesn't make sense, but it anchors you anyway.

Want to hear God clearly and consistently? Start with the Bible. His Word is a spiritual GPS that never leads you off course. The more scripture you have in you, the more the Holy Spirit can bring it to mind when you need it most (John 14:26 and Psalm 119:105).

Now, let's talk about obedience because hearing is one thing, but responding is another. Look at Ananias in Acts 9. God told him to lay hands on Saul, the same man who had been persecuting Christians. That didn't make sense in the natural, but Ananias obeyed, and it changed everything. When you obey, even in uncertainty, God can trust you with more (Acts 9:10-17).

When it comes to patience? Look at Joseph. He heard from God through dreams but didn't step into purpose overnight. There were years of betrayal, silence, and confusion. Yet, Joseph didn't rush ahead of God. And when the time was right, the vision came to pass (Genesis 41:41-44). Waiting is hard, but God's silence doesn't mean He's not working; it means He's preparing. Jesus Himself often withdrew from the crowd to hear from the Father (Luke 5:16). If the Son of God needed quiet time, you already know we do too.

How I Meditate on Scripture

One of the practical ways I've learned to meditate on God's Word is through scripture memorization. I know what it feels like to be mentally drained by the demands of career, family, and life, so I had to find simple, sustainable ways to hide God's Word in my heart. Here's what I do. I'll choose a scripture that speaks to the season I'm in or an area in which I'm struggling. I'll record myself reading that scripture aloud on my phone. Throughout the day, I'll replay that recording over and over again, whether I'm driving, cooking, or working out, until I have it memorized.

It's like training my spirit the same way you'd train your body at the gym. The more I hear it, the more it becomes part of me. The more it becomes part of me, the more it transforms my life. When I meditate on scripture, I don't stop at memorizing words. I ask questions. "What is this passage really saying?" "What does this reveal about God's character?" "How does this apply to my life right now?" "Holy Spirit, what are You trying to show me through this verse?"

Meditation is an invitation to lean in, slow down, and listen. It's how God's Word becomes alive and active. It is not just something we read, but it is something we live. For You, Woman of Cultivation, if you've been running on empty and are always busy but spiritually drained, I want to challenge you:

+ Find little moments to talk to God and acknowledge His presence in your day.

+ Choose one scripture each week and meditate on it—not just by reading it, but by reflecting on what it means for your life.

+ Record yourself reading scripture and play it while you're on the move.

+ Don't just pray. Pause and listen.

You don't need more hours in the day to draw closer to God. You need more intentional moments. Meditation is how we anchor ourselves in God's truth while the world around us keeps spinning. When you make room for prayer and meditation, you will begin to experience what Jesus meant when He said, "My sheep hear My voice, and I know them, and they follow Me" (John 10:27). You'll no longer just pray for answers. You'll learn how to hear His voice and live from a place of peace and purpose.

> ●**Real Talk Moment:**
> Heaven isn't on your to-do list. It's the destination. Don't treat time with God like a task. Treat it like a lifeline.

Career Woman Connection

If you're anything like me, a career woman, a goal-getter, and a person who is always on the move, you've probably fallen into the same routine. Quick prayers when you find a moment, a whispered "Lord, help me" on the way to work, a few words before bed. However, let me remind you that your ambition will never replace your need for intimacy with God. Your schedule might be full, but your soul can't afford to run on empty. The more you rise in your career, the more intentional you must become in your prayer life, not because God is impressed by your success but because your success will crush you without His guidance.

Cultivated BOSS Method™ Tie-In: Spirit-led

A truly cultivated woman isn't just bold in faith or obedient when it's easy; she's Spirit-led in every season. The third pillar of the Cultivated BOSS Method™ reminds us that prayer isn't about performance. It's about posture. When your heart is aligned with the Holy Spirit, your prayers become powerful, your peace becomes steady, and your direction becomes clear. You're not meant to figure it all out on your own. Let the Spirit lead.

Why Your Prayers May Feel Powerless

The Bible tells us in Matthew 15:8-9, *"These people honor me with their lips, but their hearts are far from me."* That used to be me. Maybe it's you, too. Maybe you've been honoring God with your lips, but you have been keeping your heart guarded. Sometimes, our prayers feel powerless because:

◆ We have the wrong motives.

- We're living unrighteously.
- We're harboring unforgiveness.
- It's simply not your season yet, but your harvest is still coming.
- Sometimes, it's all of the above, and we're over here wondering why God hasn't sent an Amazon Prime delivery on our blessing. However, when we, like Hannah, get honest before God, everything begins to change.

Strategies to Cultivate Effective Prayer and Meditation

Here are simple and practical strategies you can start using today to strengthen your prayer life and meditate on God's Word:

1. Schedule Your Prayer Time. – Set a specific time to pray in the morning and at night. Put it on your calendar or set an alarm for this to become apart of your daily routine.

2. Create a Dedicated Prayer Space. – Find a quiet spot where you can consistently meet with God—whether it's a corner of your room, car, or a cozy chair.

3. Start and End Your Day with Prayer. – Begin your day thanking God and surrendering your plans to Him. End your day reflecting on how He showed up and giving Him your worries.

4. Pick a Scripture to Meditate On. – Choose one Bible verse each day or week that speaks to your current need or season.

5. Write It and Keep It Visible. – Put the verse on a sticky note, your phone wallpaper, or your planner, so you see it throughout the day.

6. Record and Replay the Verse. – Record yourself reading the scripture aloud and listen to it during your commute, while cooking, or anytime you have a free moment.

7. Pause and Reflect. – Throughout the day, pause and ask: *What is God saying to me in this verse? How can I apply it today?*

8. Start with Praise and Worship. – Before you pray, play a worship song or simply thank God for who He is. This helps shift your focus from your problems to His presence.

9. Invite the Holy Spirit to Lead Your Prayers. – Don't rely on your own words. Ask the Holy Spirit to guide what you say, reveal what's on God's heart, and even help you pray in spiritual tongues if you're led.

10. Surrender Control. – End each prayer by giving God your desires, plans, and worries. Remind yourself daily that He's in control, not you.

Letting Go and Letting God Lead

Here's what I want you to take from all of this, Woman of Cultivation:

You may be a woman who's got goals, a packed calendar, and a lot of people depending on you, but don't forget that even the strongest career woman needs to stop striving and start surrendering. You can pray about your next promotion, business, relationships, and breakthrough. Still, the real breakthrough will always happen when you stop trying to control the outcome and start trusting the One who already wrote the story.

Most importantly, don't stop praying. Don't stop showing up in your prayer closet, even when it feels like nothing is changing. Don't stop talking to God just because you don't see immediate results. Don't stop meditating on His Word because you're busy chasing success. When the Bible says never cease praying, this looks like living in a constant conversation with God, whether you're riding in the car, sitting at your desk, cooking dinner, or facing a hard moment. It's turning your thoughts, worries, and even your victories into prayers throughout the day, keeping your heart open and connected to Him at all times.

Like Hannah, my breakthrough didn't come overnight. It came when I let go. It came when I realized I didn't have to carry everything on my own. It came when I learned that the prayers I prayed with tears would one day become the testimonies I shared with boldness. Psalm 1:2–3 NLT says, *"But they delight in the law of the Lord, meditating on it day and night. They are like trees planted along the riverbank, bearing fruit each season. Their leaves never wither, and they prosper in all they do."*

This is what happens when we cultivate a lifestyle of prayer and meditation. We thrive. We grow. We become unshaken by life's seasons. We shift from survival mode to surrender mode. Like Hannah and like me, you will look back one day and realize your prayers not only changed your circumstances, but they also changed you. You'll finally understand that while you were busy praying for God to change everything around you, He was actually busy working on the most important project of all—YOU. Visit www.eyfbook.com to download the "Prayer Template Pack" to deepen your prayer life and hear God more clearly.

CHAPTER 9

UNDERSTANDING WHY AND HOW TO FAST

"Even now," says the Lord, "Turn and come to Me with all your heart and genuine repentance, with fasting and weeping in mourning until every barrier is removed and the broken fellowship is restored..."
— (**Joel 2:12, AMP**)

Meet Anna:
The Woman Who Fasted and Never Gave Up

Before we dive deeper into fasting, let me introduce you to a woman in the Bible who doesn't often get the spotlight. Still, her lifestyle quietly speaks volumes to us, career-driven, busy, multitasking women. Her name is Anna the Prophetess (Luke 2:36-38). She was a widow who lived in the temple, dedicating her entire life to worship, fasting, and prayer. Scripture tells us she was married for only seven years before her husband died, and from that moment forward, she gave her whole heart to God. She was around 84 years old when she saw Jesus presented in the temple, recognizing immediately that He was the promised Messiah. She had been faithfully fasting, praying, and waiting for decades, and because of her dedication, she was one of the first to witness God's promise fulfilled. Anna's story reminds us that fasting isn't just about temporary results; it's about posture, persistence, and positioning yourself to recognize God when He shows up. Like Anna, we must be women who are willing to posture ourselves in surrender and expectation (Luke 2:36-38).

The Doorway to God's Presence: Why Fasting Matters

"I can't give up my food and drinks for too long. It'll make me sick." "I don't see the need to fast." "Fasting isn't for everybody." "God knows my heart." I used to say these things from a place of lack of knowledge. I used to have a whole list of excuses ready like a menu, except nothing on it actually fed my spirit. Honestly, I was the queen of "God knows my heart" with a side of snacks in my hands. Yes, it was true that I would get sick if I went too long without eating, but I was not fasting properly. I would automatically jump into a fast without preparing my body, so my body would crash due to a lack of carbs and sugar.

Why is fasting important? Fasting allows us to grow closer to God by denying our flesh and fueling our spirits. Fasting is when we give up food or our personal pleasures to deepen our relationship with God. When fasting is done properly, you will be more in tune with the Holy Spirit, and your connection with the spiritual realm heightens. We are weakened physically, so God can pour into us spiritually. Through fasting, we can experience breakthroughs and fresh encounters with God, unlocking God's secret wisdom and the transformation of ourselves into the kingdom women He wants us to be. You can fast for many different reasons, such as wanting to grow closer to God, desiring to be a better person, wanting to strengthen your spirit, desiring a breakthrough in a certain area of your life, or attaining better health or finances, etc.

> **🗨Real Talk Moment:**
> God knows my heart is not a fast pass to avoid fasting. If He's calling you to let go of something, He's already prepared the grace for you to endure it.

BOSS Method™ Tie-In: Spirit-led

Fasting is one of the most Spirit-led decisions you can make in your spiritual journey. It's not about a rule, it's about a response to God's invitation. As a Cultivated BOSS, being Spirit-led means allowing the Holy Spirit to guide when, how, and why you fast. It's trusting that your breakthrough doesn't come from your effort but your surrender. Let the Holy Spirit lead you, just like He led Anna, into deeper intimacy and divine clarity.

When You Empty Yourself, God Fills You Up

There are different types of fasts. With any fast, allowing the Holy Spirit to lead is best. Anna understood that a lifestyle of fasting wasn't about rules; it was about creating a lifestyle where there was room for God. Here are different types of fasts:

- Absolute Fast: Abstaining from both food and beverages for a short period, and from immediate spiritual needs. (Esther 4:15, Saul in Acts 9:8-9)

- Complete Fast: Abstaining from all food and drinking water only. (Judges 20:26)

- Daniel Fast: Abstaining from particular foods like meats, sweets, and bread. Eating fruits, vegetables, legumes, whole grains, nuts, and seeds. (Daniel 1:12; 10:2-3)

- Corporate Fast: Group fasting for a common spiritual goal. (Acts 13:2-3)

- Selective Fast: Abstaining from non-food distractions like social media or TV to spend more time with God. In 1 Corinthians 7:1-5, couples temporarily set aside physical intimacy to devote themselves more fully to prayer.

Prior to fasting, it's good to understand the "why" behind your reason for fasting and what you want to accomplish during the fast. It's a good idea to seek God out to determine which type of fast is best for your situation. If you are fasting from food, preparing your body and eating smaller meals is a good idea. Pre-fasting meals (a few days before you fast) should contain complex carbs, such as whole grains, pasta, potatoes, brown rice, etc., and you can include protein-rich foods, such as meat, beans, etc. Cutting back on caffeine and sugar is helpful as well to lessen withdrawal symptoms. Anna made fasting a lifestyle because she understood that it wasn't about temporary sacrifice. It was about long-term spiritual growth and intimacy with God.

> **●Real Talk Moment:**
> You can scroll on Instagram for 2 hours without blinking, but fasting for 3 hours feels like you've been in the wilderness for 40 days. Stay focused, your spirit is growing.

My Personal Journey: From Fear to Faith-Filled Fasting

I remember doing my first complete fast with no food, and I could only drink water for over 24 hours. It was required for my deliverance session. I was supposed to fast for five days. The first three days were a complete fast with water only from 6 am to 3 pm, which was fine with me because I was used to doing 12-hour fasts, so I knew I could do a nine-hour fast. On the fourth day, I was supposed to fast from 6 am until the following day (day 5) after my deliverance session was over, which was scheduled for 12 pm. In the past, when I would do water fasts for an extended period of time, I would get severe headaches, stomach cramps, and extreme fatigue. I feel like this was mostly because I did not prepare properly or have faith that God would see me through.

I was nervous! I remember reaching out to my spiritual mentor/ leader who would be doing my deliverance session, saying, "I'm not sure if I can fast with water only beyond 12 hours because I haven't had good experiences healthwise when trying to attempt it in the past." She told me that I could incorporate vegetables, which was a relief to me. Then, I began to think I was going to try to tough it out for as long as I could. My husband was fasting as well. He had done this sort of fast before, and he had even done a 3-day absolute fast (no water or food), so I had to know his secret. I asked him how he was able to get through his water fasts. He told me that he relied on God, tried not to even think about the fact that he hadn't eaten, and whenever hunger pains kicked in, he guzzled a bunch of water. I was looking at him in amazement. He said, "I'm telling you to rely on God by asking Him for strength. Don't think about eating and fill up on water. You can do it." That simple conversation was exactly what I needed to hear, which boosted my confidence tremendously!

> **●Real Talk Moment:**
> Don't underestimate the power of a praying husband and a whole lotta water. That combo took me from I can't to I did that! And I'm telling you, you can too!

I said, "Okay, I'm gonna try it!" I did exactly what he said when day 4 came. Whenever I felt those hunger pains kicking in, I would drink my water and pray to God for the strength to endure the hunger pains I felt. I also found myself thanking Him and praying for whatever else came to mind. Before I knew it, I had made it through 16 hours of fasting prior to going to bed. When I woke up the next morning on day five, I had made it past 24 hours and felt so accomplished. I couldn't wait to let my spiritual leader know that I didn't need the vegetables after all. She was proud that I had pushed through, and my husband was also proud of me. By experiencing the grace of God, having a supportive husband, and realizing I had a chance to overcome my fears and doubts, I was able to overcome my negative thoughts of fasting for extended periods of time.

My faith and relationship with God increased as well because I allowed Him to take full control of the situation. I also had a smooth deliverance session because I allowed myself to be open to what God was trying to do. I have done a few 24-hour fasts on my own since then. Plus, I've made fasting a part of my lifestyle whenever I feel led to do so.

While writing this book, I also find myself naturally falling into a pattern of fasting from food, but I still have my water and coffee from early in the morning until late afternoon or evening. Sometimes, I cut coffee out completely and just have water and no food. I notice that during these times, I am able to think clearly, focus, and get my thoughts out on paper without feeling mentally clogged. It's funny how a little hunger will clear your mind really quickly. It turns out that my creativity doesn't run on carbs—it runs on coffee and the Holy Spirit! In all seriousness, the Holy Spirit is truly the one to credit for the clarity and flow that came during those fasting hours. I've even heard pastors say before that food can clog us up, both spiritually and physically. It became clear to me that when I denied my flesh even in this way, it gave God space to pour into me creatively and spiritually.

Fasting can be difficult, but when we accomplish it with good intentions, there is power behind it. When you have faith and believe that God will see you through, you can accomplish the things you thought were impossible.

The Power in Pressing Through

Anna's story is a reminder that fasting is not a quick fix but a posture of surrender and expectation. She spent years fasting and praying, and when she finally saw Jesus in the temple, her heart's desire was fulfilled. When I tried to complete a fast I thought was impossible, I kept telling myself that I could do it, and I did, with the help of my Lord and Savior. I encourage you to go deeper with God through fasting, so you too can experience God on a new level. Imagine your flesh acting like a toddler throwing a tantrum because it's not getting snacks, but your spirit is growing stronger with every "no" you say to yourself. Fasting teaches you that breakthrough isn't about striving, it's about surrendering, and on the other side of that surrender is a deeper intimacy with the One who satisfies beyond food, comfort, or control.

> 💬 **Real Talk Moment:**
> Your flesh will act up like a kid who just got their screen time taken away. Know that your spirit gets stronger every time you say no to it.

Keys to Cultivating a Fasting Lifestyle

Here are some strategies and tips to help you grow deeper into your fasting journey:

1. Think about one small way you could start fasting regularly. – Could you skip breakfast once a week to pray? Could you give

up your afternoon coffee run and use that time to talk with God? Start simple and create space in your busy schedule to hear from Him more clearly.

2. Shift your mindset to actively look for God to show up during your fast. – Expect Him to speak, guide, and reveal things, even if it's not in the way you imagined. He always delivers, just in His perfect way and timing.

3. Look over the different fasting methods and ask God which one fits your current season. – What area of your life needs surrender? What could you set aside, whether it is food or distractions, to make space for God to move?

4. Prepare your body. – Start eating smaller, lighter meals with complex carbs and protein-rich foods a few days before your fast. Cut back on sugar and caffeine, so your body isn't shocked when you begin fasting.

5. Commit and be intentional. – Write down why you're fasting, what you're giving up, and when you'll fast. Put it on your calendar like an important appointment with God.

6. Set aside intentional moments during your fast to pray, meditate, and journal. – Pick a scripture each day, read it slowly, and write down what God is showing you.

7. Notice how you feel during your fast, whether it's frustration, doubt, or hunger pains, and take a moment to talk to God about it. – Write down one thing you're grateful for each time you feel challenged.

8. If fasting is new to you, ease into it. – Start with a short fast like skipping one meal, and always check with a medical provider first if you have health concerns.

Your Fasting Lifestyle Begins Now

Matthew 6:16-18 ESV reminds us, *"And when you fast, do not look gloomy like the hypocrites... But when you fast, anoint your head and wash your face... And your Father who sees in secret will reward you."* Fasting may seem daunting at first, but if you leave it to God and have faith that you can do it with His help, He will equip you with what you need to endure the process. If you are ready to move forward with the deep things of God, receive breakthroughs, and increase your spiritual gifts/awareness, then it's time to fast. The benefits will be well worth it in the end.

Don't just read this chapter and nod your head. Make a decision today. Whether it's skipping a meal once a week to spend time with God or giving up social media for a week, start somewhere. You're not just a woman with a career or a profession. You are a woman on assignment; fasting will keep you spiritually sharp for the assignment ahead.

> **💬Real Talk Moment:**
> Don't wait for the perfect time to fast. If you can schedule a nail appointment, you can schedule a spiritual one too.

As a career woman, I want to encourage you to look at fasting not as a burden, but as a beautiful invitation into God's presence. Fasting is not reserved for the super spiritual or those who have extra time. It's for busy women like you and me, women who carry responsibilities, goals, and big dreams. If Anna the Prophetess could fast and pray well into her eighties, and I can fast while raising a family, writing a book, and trying not to snack every five minutes, you can too. When you choose to make fasting part of your lifestyle, even in small, consistent ways, you'll discover clarity, renewed energy, and a Divine strategy like never before. You don't have to strive or perform; you simply have to show up surrendered. God will meet you in the sacrifice and pour back into you more than you ever gave up. I've created a resource to help simplify fasting for you. Visit www.eyfbook.com to download the "Fasting & Faith Strategy Guide" to help you prepare spiritually and experience a breakthrough through biblical fasting.

CHAPTER 10
REDISCOVER VALUES AND VISIONS

"Where there is no vision, the people perish: but he that keepeth the law, happy is he."
(Proverbs 29:18 KJV)

You Are Seen: The Woman in the Wilderness

Before we dive into the concept of vision and values, let's begin with a woman who lost her way, literally and spiritually, but God saw her. Her name was Hagar. She wasn't a queen or prophetess. She wasn't the one people expected God to speak to. Hagar was an Egyptian slave caught in the middle of someone else's plan. She was used, discarded, and then left to fend for herself with a child on the way. When Hagar ran away into the wilderness, she wasn't just physically lost. She was emotionally and spiritually wandering, trying to figure out who she was and where she belonged, but in that barren place, God showed up. He didn't wait until she "had it all together." He met her in her confusion, pain, and isolation.

He called her by name. He saw her. He gave her a vision, and Hagar became the first person in the Bible to name God. She called God "El Roi," meaning the God who sees me (Genesis 16:13). You may be reading this and feel like you've been wandering, too, trying to figure out who you really are outside of your career, titles, family roles, or the opinions of others. You may have been running from rejection, regret, or even from yourself, but here's the truth. God sees you. Right here. Right now. No, He's not waiting until you get that next degree, lose 10 pounds, or finally figure out how to organize your prayer closet. He sees you now in the messy middle of it all.

Where Is Your Life Headed?

This was the question I had to let marinate a few years ago. Imagine yourself on a city bus, wondering where it's headed. You've already made the stop for your career, but now the bus is just traveling aimlessly. Hagar, too, found herself on an "aimless bus ride," running without a clear destination and feeling lost and discarded, but God redirected her. Some of you may feel like you're on a Greyhound to nowhere with a bag full of burdens and no GPS. I've been there too.

> 💬**Real Talk Moment:**
> You're not just on a bus to nowhere, you're in the middle of a God-ordained reroute. Buckle up, Woman of God. This detour has destiny written all over it.

What Is Vision? — A Divine Perspective

The dictionary defines vision as a state of being able to see, or the ability to imagine and plan the future. Still, according to the Bible, vision is when God reveals secret knowledge or Divine insight to you. Hagar didn't expect to receive a vision in the wilderness, but that's where she met God. He gave her direction and reassurance that her child's future was in His hands. Specifically, God told Hagar in Genesis 16:11-12 that she would give birth to a son named Ishmael, meaning "God hears," and he would become the father of a great nation. Though it wasn't the prettiest promise, it was a clear vision of her future and confirmation that her life and her child's life mattered.

> 💬**Real Talk Moment:**
> That wilderness might feel like a delay, but it's actually Divine direction in disguise.

In a similar way, I received my vision during what felt like a dry and uncertain season. It wasn't through a dramatic dream or a booming voice from heaven. It was a simple, undeniable moment. One night, I saw a miniature tree floating in my bedroom. That small image carried a big message: God was calling me to plant seeds of faith and watch them grow through the words I would write.

Understand that it will not always be comfortable when God reveals His vision for your life. Hagar didn't receive comforting words; she was told to return to her difficult circumstances, but she was equipped with the knowledge that God saw her and had a future for her. If you're wondering how to discover God's vision for your life, here are a few ways to start:

- Spend intentional time in prayer, specifically asking God to reveal His plans and purpose for you.

- Immerse yourself in the Word of God. It is full of His promises and direction.

- Pay attention to patterns, confirmations, or repeated themes God may show you through scripture, people, dreams, or even circumstances.

- Seek wise, godly counsel who can help affirm what you're sensing.

- Consider fasting and quieting outside noise, so you can hear Him clearly.

What Are Values? — Anchoring Yourself

Values are the standards or beliefs we consider essential in life. My top three are love, faith, and authenticity. I chose love because it's the foundation of everything God asks of me: to love Him wholeheartedly and extend that same love to others. I chose faith because it's impossible to please God without faith, and I need faith to navigate life's uncertainties. I chose authenticity because I've spent too many years living to please others, wearing masks, and hiding who I truly am. Now, I want to show up fully as the woman God created me to be. Hagar didn't have the privilege of setting her own values in the beginning. She was living under Sarah and Abraham's decisions, not her own. However, after her encounter with God, she realized her worth and the value of being seen.

When I Settled for Less

Growing up, I never thought about my values. My original plan was to go to school to be a neonatologist, but I ended up in nursing because of transportation issues. When I look back, I realize I wasn't being intentional about my values or my vision. I was doing what most of us were taught after high school—go to college, and if you don't, get a good job and figure out the rest later. Hagar was forced into a life she didn't choose. She was told what to do, how to live, and where to go, but God stepped in and revealed that her life had more meaning than her circumstances suggested.

A Funny Wake-Up Call

A funny story I remember is, years ago, when I used to work for a health insurance company as a registered nurse. One morning, I was playing this rap song in the car that had a ton of cussing in it. Before I pulled up to work, I made sure to turn it down, so no one would hear it. When I got to my cubicle, my hands were full of stuff. Somehow, a button got pressed on my phone, and the next thing you know, the song was blaring. All I heard was, "Walk around the clubbbb..." and I knew the next words were curse words after curse words.

I moved faster than ever during a code blue at the hospital. It was like the Holy Spirit gave me superhuman speed. People were laughing as I rushed to turn the song off. When I finally turned the song off, I laughed, like, *I'm not sure where that came from,* knowing good and well I was just pounding it before coming in. I knew exactly where it came from. It came from my own personal party of one, right there in my car. I was basically DJ'ing for the devil on my drive to work through the week and lifting my hands in praise on Sundays. Make it make sense!

The False Identity Trap

That moment was funny, but it was also revealing. I realized I had been living a double life. I was playing vulgar music one minute, praising God the next. I was carrying a false identity. Here's the thing. What we consume affects us. Listening to music full of cussing, degrading language, and negativity doesn't just sit in our ears. It settles in our spirits. It influences how we think, speak, see ourselves, and posture ourselves before God.

> 💬**Real Talk Moment:**
> What you consistently play in your ears can start to influence how you think, how you feel, and how you live.

You may not realize it at the moment, but that music-the kind that glorifies violence, promiscuity, disrespect, and language that doesn't honor God—slowly shapes your attitude, language, mood, and spiritual posture. It can make you numb to the very things you're trying to overcome. It can make it harder to hear God's voice clearly because there's too much static from the world in your ears. Pause and ask yourself: *What noise have I been allowing into my spirit that's been drowning out God's voice?* Hagar's story reminds us that clarity comes when we step away from the noise and let God meet us in the wilderness.

Rediscovering Yourself in the Wilderness

The enemy will always try to pull us away from who God says we are. We can't have one foot in the church and one foot in the world, and wonder why we're always exhausted, but the wilderness isn't the end. It's the place where God meets you to rewrite your story. Who told you who you were? Was it God, or was it your ex, your boss, social media, or that voice in your head telling you you're not enough? If you've been letting broken people, social media, or your past tell you who you are, it's time to change your source.

> 💬**Real Talk Moment:**
> You've been scrolling for answers when you should be searching the Scriptures.

Hagar rediscovered herself when she realized that God saw her. Remembering that God sees you too, you will rediscover your values and vision. You may feel like the most overlooked, unseen woman in the room, but if God saw Hagar, an outsider in the wilderness, He absolutely sees you right now.

Tangible Strategies to Rediscover God's Vision & Your Values

Here are some ways you can rediscover God's visions and values for your life:

1. Do a 10-Minute Daily Vision Check-In. – Set aside 10 quiet minutes each day to pray and ask God: *What are You calling me to do in this season?* Write down any thoughts, scriptures, or impressions that come to mind.

2. Rediscover Your Values. – Write down ten things that matter most to you, then circle your top three. Ask yourself: *Are my choices reflecting these values?* If not, choose one small step you can take this week to realign with what matters most.

3. Do a Time & Attention Audit. – Track how you spend your time and energy for one full day. At the end of the day, ask yourself: *Did how I spent my time reflect what I say I value?*

4. Fast from One Distraction for 3 Days. – Choose one thing pulling you away from God (social media, TV, certain music, etc.). For three days, fast from it and use that time to pray, read scripture, or journal.

5. Write a Surrender Letter to God. – Write a letter listing everything you've been prioritizing above God: career, relationships, money, etc. End the letter by surrendering those things and asking Him to reveal His vision for your life.

6. Reflect on Your Wilderness Season. – Think back to a difficult season in your life. Ask yourself: *What did God teach me during that time? How did it shape my values or direction?* Write down what He revealed to you in that wilderness moment.

Keep Moving Toward Clarity

These simple but powerful strategies aren't about adding more to your to-do list. They're about helping you slow down, listen, and realign your life with what truly matters. I want you to realize your answers may not come right away, and you must wait with expectancy, believing that God will reveal it all in due time. Just like Hagar discovered in the wilderness, God has a vision for your life, even when you can't see it yet. As you take these small steps, trust that He will begin to reveal the bigger picture. You don't have to figure it all out today. Your only job is to stay open, surrender, and let God lead the way.

BOSS Method™ Tie-In: Strategic for Kingdom Impact

Rediscovering your vision and values is more than self-reflection; it's Kingdom strategy. The final pillar of the Cultivated BOSS Method™ is Strategic for Kingdom Impact. When you seek God for vision and anchor your life in His values, you start making Spirit-led decisions that ripple beyond your personal life. Strategy means every step you take is intentional, not accidental. You're not just living, you're building. You're planting Kingdom seeds that produce real fruit, on purpose.

When Heartbreak Breaks Your Vision

One of the turning points where I realized I had no clear values or vision was after a breakup that left me completely emotionally and spiritually drained. Hagar's wilderness moment wasn't just physical. It was emotional and filled with heartbreak, rejection, and isolation. I found myself in that same wilderness after this breakup. My older sister and I attended church regularly and wanted to get more involved. We decided to join the church choir, which was a big deal because we attended a large Baptist church. We were thrilled to be part of something meaningful, meeting weekly for rehearsals and singing on Sunday mornings. Everyone in the choir seemed to get along well, and I felt like I had finally found my place.

At that point, you couldn't tell me anything. I just knew I was on the fast track to a spiritual promotion! Then, I met a band member who was also charming, and we started dating. Early on, he told me that he used to have a deep relationship with God, but he had drifted away. That should have been my cue to run the other way, but I brushed it off, thinking, *no one is perfect, and he's a nice guy.* Another red flag I ignored was that I had just gotten out of a toxic relationship, and I was a couple of months pregnant with my daughter. Looking back, I wish I could go back and shake the mess out of the younger version of myself to wake up!

If I could time travel, I'd snatch myself by the collar and say, "Ma'am, please sit down somewhere!"

●**Real Talk Moment**:
That version of you didn't know better, but you do now. Growth looks good on you.

We dated for a couple of years, and I truly believed he was "the one." He was there for my daughter's birth, and he treated her as his own, but he had a female best friend, and although she lived far away, something about their dynamic never sat right with me.

One day, he dropped off a gift for me. I believe it was a purse as I pulled it out of the bag and noticed a few extra receipts inside. One was from my gift, but the other two caught my attention. One was from a restaurant that looked like a meal for two, and the other was for a pair of shoes. I'm still not sure how those receipts ended up in my gift bag. Maybe it was an accident or Divine intervention, because what's done in the dark will eventually be brought to the light. It was almost as if God was saying, "You're not going to stay blind to this."

My gut told me something was off, so I called him. He seemed just as confused as I was at first, then he quickly explained that he had taken his sister out for lunch and bought her some shoes, but the dates, times, and details of his story didn't add up. I put on my private eye hat (as many women do when something feels off) and began to investigate. With the amount of evidence I had, he eventually came clean. He had been messing around with someone else, and guess who it was? *Nope*, not his female best friend, but another woman, and guess where she was from? *Our church choir!* The deception hit on multiple levels.

Everything was a mess. I confronted her (which I don't recommend because it only makes things worse), and of course, she denied it, but he had already admitted the truth. I was heartbroken, disrespected, and completely crushed. To make things worse, I had to be around them at church, at choir practice, and during meetings. It was a living nightmare. I felt a lot like Hagar—betrayed, abandoned, disrespected, and forced to navigate a wilderness I didn't ask to be in.

My mindset shifted into defense mode. Can I be transparent? I was in a dark place. I felt completely betrayed, humiliated, and blindsided. Human nature kicks in when you're in that kind of emotional state. You start thinking about how to get even. You want the people who hurt you to feel what you felt. It's almost instinctual. You want to make them pay, but here's the thing. When we are responding from a place of hurt, our mindset at the time is not to care about the outcome. All we want is relief from the pain, but we have to care enough about what could potentially happen if we react in negative ways. Our reactions in those moments can cause lasting consequences, not only for others but for ourselves.

This is how vision gets blurred. This is how values get tossed aside. I want you to pause right here and reflect. Think about a time when you reacted from a place of pain. *What did it cost you? Did it bring you closer to God, or did it pull you further away from Him?*

When we don't have a strong grip on our values and when we're not clear about who we are and what God says about us, we're more likely to react out of pain instead of responding with wisdom. We're more likely to allow emotions to steer the bus and drive us completely off course. That's why it's crucial to know your values. Knowing your values gives you an anchor when the storms of life hit.

Your values become your filter, your compass, and your guardrails. They remind you who you are when life tries to tell you otherwise. They protect your vision, so you won't stray from it when betrayal, heartbreak, or offense comes knocking. If I had been spiritually right with God at the time, I would've handled it differently. I would've fallen to my knees instead of letting my flesh lead the way. I would've brought my broken heart to God immediately, asking Him to heal me, guide me, and show me how to forgive rather than plot revenge. I would've guarded my heart, asked the Holy Spirit to help me see clearly, and leaned into God's peace instead of reacting in offense.

I had to lean on Him because the pain, betrayal, and anger were overwhelming. I wrestled with church hurt, questioning how true believers in Christ could do something like this, but then I remembered the words of my pastor. "The church is a house for the sick. We all need Jesus." That truth hit me hard. I realized that just because people attend church doesn't mean they are spiritually whole. We are all in need of healing and grace, and just like Hagar, I had to face the reality that even though people had used and discarded me, God saw me. He called me by name, met me in the wilderness, and reminded me that my story wasn't over, and with time, that's exactly what He did.

I've come to forgive them both, and no, I don't wish any ill will toward either of them. I pray that they have gotten right with God and have forgiven themselves regarding the matter. You know you're maturing in Christ when you can think about someone who hurt you, and your first instinct is to pray for them instead of plot on them, and I'm not talking about the backhanded "I'm gonna pray for you" comment when secretly you're saying it from a dark place. It's a sincere statement coming from a good place with a humble heart. If you're carrying betrayal, offense, or rejection right now, let this be your wake-up call. Your healing is waiting on the other side of forgiveness.

How You Know You've Truly Forgiven Someone

- You can think about the situation without feeling the same level of pain or bitterness.
- You no longer desire revenge or wish them harm.
- You can pray for them and mean it.
- You release the need for an apology or explanation.
- You focus more on your healing than their punishment.

> **Real Talk Moment:**
> Forgiveness doesn't mean you approve of what they did. It means you're choosing peace over poison.

Your Wilderness Is Not the End

Psalm 37:4 says, *"Delight yourself in the Lord, and He will give you the desires of your heart."* This means finding your ultimate joy and great pleasure in your relationship with God and aligning your desires with His will because He is the central focus of your happiness. You don't have to stay lost, wandering, or weighed down by who the world says you are. Just like Hagar, you may have found yourself in a wilderness you didn't choose, but you are not forgotten. God sees you. He knows you by name. He has a vision for your life, even when you feel discarded, overlooked, or broken.

Rediscovering your visions and values is essential to your walk with Christ. You begin to move differently when you understand who you are in Him and what truly matters. You will stop letting circumstances, people, or emotions steer your life and instead allow God's voice to lead you. Knowing your values will help you stand firm when life tries to knock you off course, and having a clear vision will give you the confidence to step boldly into the future God has prepared for you.

> **●Real Talk Moment:**
> You might've felt invisible, but Heaven's been watching the whole time, and God's got receipts.

Here's my challenge to you. Don't leave this chapter without pausing and asking yourself, *What do I value? What vision has God placed in my heart? Am I living in alignment with it?*

Your future depends on how you answer those questions. You are not the mistakes of your past. You are not the labels others have placed on you. You are a woman who is seen, loved, and called by God. I've created a resource to help you rediscover what is essential in your life. Visit www.eyfbook.com to download the "Kingdom Vision & Core Values Mapping Sheet" to help you clarify your vision, redefine your values, and align your life with God's plan. Your story isn't over. It's just getting started.

CHAPTER 11
SET NEW GOALS AND PUT FAITH INTO ACTION

*"Blessed is she who has believed that the
Lord would fulfill his promises to her."*
(Luke 1:45 NIV)

The Bold Faith of a Desperate Woman

Faith is powerful. It's bold, barrier-breaking, and life-shifting. No one shows us this better than the Canaanite woman. She wasn't supposed to belong. She wasn't part of the religious "in crowd." She was an outsider, a Gentile, a woman dismissed by culture, but she had a need so desperate that it pushed her past fear, rejection, and shame. Her daughter was suffering terribly, tormented by an unclean spirit (Matthew 15:22). Can you imagine the sleepless nights and the helplessness of watching your child suffer without relief? That kind of desperation will make you forget what people think, so she came to Jesus, crying out for mercy.

At first, Jesus said nothing. The disciples wanted her gone, and when Jesus finally spoke, He said He was only sent to the lost sheep of Israel, but she didn't stop there. She knelt before Him and said, "Lord, help me." Even when He replied, "It is not right to take the children's bread and toss it to the dogs," she stayed persistent. She said, "Even the dogs eat the crumbs that fall from their master's table." That was her moment. Jesus looked at her and said, "Woman, you have great faith! Your request is granted." Her daughter, who had been tormented by a demon, was healed that very hour. She didn't let rejection, silence, or public opinion stop her. She fought for her daughter's deliverance. That's what dominion looks like. She basically said, "You can call me what you want, but I'm not leaving without my blessing!" (Matthew 15:21-28).

> 🍷**Real Talk Moment**:
> Don't let people's opinions punk you out of your blessing. That woman didn't care who was watching. She came for her miracle and refused to leave empty-handed.

A Dream Turned Vision: Your Assignment Is Strategic

Reading her story made me reflect on how strategic God is when He places us on Earth. Not long ago, I had a dream that turned into a vision—a Divine encounter that revealed how intentional God is about our assignments. It started like any normal dream. My husband and I were throwing a huge house party but we were not in our current home. We were in a massive mansion. It was so big that I could barely find my husband in the crowd. It felt extravagant, noisy, and chaotic. It was like I was hosting a party I didn't even want to be at. You know the party's too big when you can't even find the person you threw it with!

Eventually, I started kicking everyone out. Something in me knew the atmosphere wasn't right. Then, once I was downstairs alone, a man appeared, trying to seduce me. I told him firmly, "I can't sleep with you. I'm married," but something was off. This wasn't about the man. I realized I wasn't dealing with flesh and blood. I was dealing with a spirit. Calmly, I said, "Spirit of fear and anxiety, go back to the dry places you came from. I want you up and out now in the name of Jesus." The spirit left instantly. His body became disfigured like a hollow shell without a soul. It was almost like the skeleton had been removed, leaving behind a flimsy, lifeless pile of flesh. A spirit of fear and anxiety can lead to sexual promiscuity when people seek comfort or validation in unhealthy relationships. Instead of finding identity in God, fear drives them to chase temporary intimacy to soothe deep emotional voids.

After I called the first spirit out, more spirits began appearing with human form shells. Each one was unique, carrying a different unclean spirit. One of them stood in front of a microphone, listing its characteristics. I knew immediately it was the spirit of anger. It felt like something was caught in my throat, keeping me from speaking, but I kept pushing through until I declared, "Spirit of anger, come out in the name of Jesus!" It fled. Again, just a shell was left behind. There were others who were waiting in line, but before I could confront them, the scene shifted.

Suddenly, I was in a vision but didn't realize it until the end. I was in outer space. It was like I was in some sort of room. The room had a massive glass window, and I could see the entire Earth below me. It was like I was looking at a giant map of the U.S.A. There was someone standing next to me, although I couldn't make out who it was. They stood at a control panel on the wall, pressing buttons. As I looked down, a glowing green map with a red target circle hovering over Indiana appeared. Then, I began moving, zooming in fast, like lightning, from the U.S. to Indiana, then Indianapolis, then to my neighborhood, and then to my house. I was seeing everything through the eyes of myself as if I had become the map itself, being drawn in closer and closer.

I remember seeing Monument Circle and downtown Indy as I passed by. I asked the Holy Spirit to slow down because I wanted to see where we were going. Then, I arrived right at my home. As I started to drop down toward my house, I told the Holy Spirit, "Noooo!" I wasn't ready to go back. I wanted to see more, but I felt myself falling. It was dark, but I knew I was returning to my body. I felt my soul land gently back into my body like a soft thud. I woke up and thought to myself, *I just had an out-of-body experience.*

It may sound wild, but Biblically, it's not unheard of. The prophet Ezekiel was carried in visions to faraway places (Ezekiel 8:3). The Apostle Paul wrote about being caught up to the third heaven (2 Corinthians 12:2). John the Revelator was transported in the Spirit to receive visions (Revelation 4:1-2). That dream wasn't random. It was a wake-up call that Heaven sends us here strategically with pre-assigned missions. My assignment in that dream was clear. I was sent to call out unclean spirits, free people, and move in spiritual authority. The truth is that you have an assignment too.

> 💬**Real Talk Moment:**
> Some parties you weren't meant to host. When the atmosphere shifts, don't stay out of politeness, clean house, and make room for God's presence.

The Kind of Faith That Moves Mountains

A couple of years prior to my previous dream and vision, I had another supernatural encounter—one that taught me how relentless the enemy is when you're getting closer to God. It was one of those days when I had spent hours praying, studying God's Word, and soaking in His presence. I felt strong, expectant, and on fire. I even prayed specifically that God would release me from anything negative holding me back, so I would walk boldly in His will. That night, around 2:00 AM, I couldn't sleep. Maybe you've had nights like that when you've been pressing in and praying for a breakthrough. I could feel something heavy in the atmosphere. It's like something was stirring, but I couldn't quite put my finger on it.

I lay there awake, feeling like something in the spirit realm was about to reveal itself, and I was right. I felt a dark presence in my room. I could see something moving back and forth at the foot of my bed. It darted rapidly from side to side, as if crawling on all fours, but I could only see its back—whatever it was. My spirit knew something had entered the room, and it wasn't friendly. Imagine this. You're lying in bed at night, finally at peace after a long day. You've prayed. You've been intentional about growing closer to God. Then, in the stillness of night, you sense something trying to disturb your peace. Suddenly, peace fades, and you find yourself in a silent war you didn't expect.

That's what it felt like. Then, I saw them. Seven or eight unclean spirits were lined up beside my bed like an army of intimidation, mocking me, taunting me. They looked as if they had Halloween masks on, but this was their actual appearance. Each one had a distorted face and different shapes and heights, and they had a darkness that radiated from them. I tried to speak to rebuke them, but I couldn't get the words out. It felt like I was stuck, paralyzed, and unable to fight back. Something inside me wouldn't let me give up. Finally, after struggling, I felt strength rise in me. I sat up, and my spirit rose high above them—so high I was standing as tall as my bedroom ceilings. I leaned in close, stared them down, and shouted, "I will not be intimidated by rulers of darkness! I rebuke you in the name of Jesus!" Just like that, their power broke. They leaned back, shrank, and vanished into thin air.

I thanked the Lord right then and there for giving me the courage to stand up to them. I was not consumed. I was in control with Jesus on my side. The enemy wants to frighten us. He wants us to live small and scared, but the more he tries to intimidate you, the more it proves how much of a threat you are. Just like the Canaanite woman, she pressed in harder when the odds were against her. She wouldn't back down. Neither will I, and neither should you.

What's wild is how the enemy will do everything in his power to stop you from stepping into that assignment. When I accepted the call to write this book, fear and anxiety tried to paralyze me. I wondered if I was qualified, if anyone would listen, and if I had what it takes. Here's what I've learned. The enemy only attacks what threatens him. I knew I must've been moving in the right direction, which was closer to God, if the enemy was sending his minions to try and intimidate me, discourage me, and deter me from what God had for me. Instead of shrinking back, it only made me want to press in more. The enemy wants us to stay frightened, confused, and stuck in spiritual stagnation, but we can rise above it. Satan's goal isn't just to distract you; he wants to destroy your faith because he knows that if he can weaken your faith, he can stop you from moving forward into the life God has called you to live. He wants to steal your confidence, shatter your belief, and keep you questioning if you're really called, but you have the authority to fight back. The stronger your faith grows, the weaker his grip becomes.

💬Real Talk Moment:
If the enemy's hitting you hard, it's probably because he sees what's coming. Hell gets nervous when Heaven's assignment is on your life.

Overcoming Fear & Anxiety When God Calls You

Let's be honest. Fear doesn't always show up in the form of monsters beside your bed. Sometimes, it shows up in real life. It can be that nervous feeling before you speak up in a meeting or the overwhelming anxiety that hits when you know God is telling you to apply for that promotion, but doubt creeps in. It might be the paralyzing fear that tells you you're not qualified to start the business, ministry, or write the book, or that middle-of-the-night voice whispering, "Who do you think you are?" The enemy knows that if he can get you to be afraid, he can keep you from moving. He'll send thoughts like: *You're not good enough. You're too late. You'll fail if you try.*

That's why the Bible says in 2 Corinthians 10:5 to take every thought captive and make it obedient to Christ, because not every thought is your thought. The enemy's goal is to plant seeds of fear, insecurity, anxiety, and doubt, so you stay stuck. The truth is that you have authority over fear. Every time fear or anxiety shows up, you have a choice. You can listen to it or speak back and say, "Not today."

♥Real Talk Moment:
Fear doesn't mean you're weak. It just means the enemy's trying to shut you up before you open your mouth and shake something.

Moment of Reflection

- *Where has fear or anxiety been showing up in your life?*
- *What random, negative thoughts have you been entertaining that are not even yours?*
- *What steps can you take today to fight back with faith?*
- *Listen, you've got enough to do without babysitting fear and anxiety like uninvited guests at your dinner table.*

Discover Your Spiritual Gifts—They're Part of Your Assignment

When God sends you, He doesn't send you empty-handed. He equips you with spiritual gifts—supernatural abilities to fulfill your Kingdom assignment. The Apostle Paul describes these gifts in 1 Corinthians 12: wisdom, teaching, leadership, discernment, faith, healing, prophecy, and more. As I've written this book and reflected on my personal stories, God has made it clear what some of my spiritual gifts are:

+ Teaching

+ Discernment

+ Wisdom

+ Encouragement

+ Faith

+ Giving

+ Deliverance and intercession

> 🗩**Real Talk Moment:**
> Your gifts aren't just cute personality traits. They're Heaven's toolkit, custom-packed for your assignment.

These gifts weren't given to me just for me. They were given so I could help you and many other women walk boldly in their assignments. You have gifts too, and you may be wondering how you can also discover your spiritual gifts. Here is what I recommend. Pray and ask God to reveal them, pay attention to what lights you up when you're serving others, and notice what people naturally come to you for.

Cultivated BOSS Method™ Tie-In: Strategic for Kingdom Impact.

It's not enough to believe; you must also build. The final pillar of the Cultivated BOSS Method™ is Strategic for Kingdom Impact because faith requires action. Just like the Canaanite woman pressed through the crowd, you must move with intentionality toward the vision God has given you. The strategy isn't yours alone. It's Holy Spirit-led. Your assignment is too important to wing it. It's time to align your goals, gifts, and calendar with your calling and walk it out like the Kingdom woman you were created to be.

Your Faith in Action: Strategies for Walking It Out

Now that you know God has assigned, gifted, and given you authority, it's time to move. Here are eight simple, tangible strategies to help you put your faith into action without feeling overwhelmed:

1. Expand Your Perspective. – When obstacles appear, remind yourself that *God is doing more than you can see.* Write one thing daily that you believe God is working on behind the scenes.

2. Ask the Holy Spirit Daily. – Spend 5–10 quiet minutes each day asking: *Holy Spirit, what's blocking me from hearing You?*

3. Say Yes to God's Assignment. – When God reveals what He wants you to do, say YES, even if you feel unqualified.

4. Pay Attention to Repeated Nudges. – If an idea, burden, or dream keeps popping up, it's likely the Holy Spirit prompting you. Write it down and start praying over it.

5. Start Small & Move. – Don't wait to have it all figured out. Take one small action toward your God-given vision, even if it's offering your service for free at first.

6. Set Spirit-led Goals. – Write three clear, God-aligned goals. Ask yourself: *Is this what God wants or what I want?*

7. Be Open to Change. – Leave room for God to redirect you. Don't cling so tightly to your plan that you miss His plan.

8. Take One Bold Step Weekly. – Every week, challenge yourself to do one thing that stretches your faith, whether it's sending an email, launching an idea, or speaking up.

> **●Real Talk Moment:**
> Stop waiting for the perfect moment. Start where you are. God moves when you move, even if it's messy.

When You Surrender the Idol, God Fulfills the Promise

I have to pause right here and let you in on something that just happened, because when I tell you God is faithful... I mean it with every fiber of my being. So there I was, sitting in my office, trying to find some help for my book campaign (yes, for this very book you're reading), reaching out to people, brainstorming content, and working on my book launch strategies. My focus was on the assignment God had already placed in front of me. My mind wasn't even thinking about school, and then my phone rang.

I glanced down at the screen, and my heart skipped. The name that popped up was someone from the university I had applied to last fall for the CRNA program, you know, the very program I told you about at the beginning of this book? The one I had been idolizing before I finally surrendered it to God? *Yep, that program.* I applied last fall for a start time of May the following year. If you're waitlisted, they have all the way up until the start of the program to call you off the waitlist.

I stared at the phone like... *Now I know she's not calling me for what I think she's calling me for.*

I picked up the phone and greeted her by name, trying to stay calm while my spirit was doing somersaults.

We exchanged a little small talk before she paused and said, "Well, I know you've been waiting a while to get into school, and I just wanted to call and let you know... you're next in line on the waitlist, and we want to offer you a spot in the program."

My mouth was probably hanging wide open at this point! I was in total disbelief. I even told her, "You definitely have caught me by surprise!" I explained that I would need to pray and seek God about it (ha—normally I wouldn't even mention needing to seek the Lord out loud when making big decisions on the spot like that, but honestly, I didn't care). I also needed to talk with my husband, because we were not planning for me to attend school this particular year. Honestly, part of me wanted to blurt out, "You're joking me, right?!" For the past two years, I had waited with full expectancy, constantly checking my email, clinging to hope, believing I would get a call, and nothing, *but this year?* The year I wasn't even focused on it. The year

I was working on my divine assignment, writing a book and building a brand. That's when I get an unexpected call offering me a spot?!

Deep down, I knew it wasn't her, and it wasn't the school. It was God's perfect timing. School was set to begin in just nineteen days. *Nineteen!* Here I was, finishing my book, planning my campaign, creating social media content, and reaching out to potential collaborators while trying to stay sane. It already felt like my plate was full, and now God had just dropped a whole new course onto the table.

To make things even more overwhelming, the school's curriculum had changed, and I didn't know any of the updates. I hadn't seen a schedule. I hadn't applied for financial aid. It definitely felt like a lot. Then it hit me: God doesn't put more on you than you can bear, and He never calls you into something expecting you to do it in your own strength. When I tell you I had surrendered CRNA school to God, I *surrendered* it. This third time around, I didn't hound the administrative office checking on my application update or reminding them that I was still waiting. I deleted the group chats where people who had applied would post nonstop updates. For two years straight, I had been on an emotional rollercoaster: "Has anybody heard anything yet?" "Did they finish interviewing?" "I got accepted!" "I'm still hoping for a call..."

Of course, if someone posted they got in, the comments would blow up with, "Congratulations! If you don't mind me asking, what are your stats?"—meaning, what kind of ICU experience they had, how strong their application was, and basically what everyone else was up against. It was exhausting. So this third time, I stopped obsessing. I stopped refreshing my email. I stopped letting it drain me. Sure, it would still come up in conversations here and there, but my answer was simple. I would tell people, "I put it in God's hands. We'll see what happens."

When Surrender Meets Resurrection

We have to depend on the Holy Spirit. That's the only way we carry divine assignments without crumbling under their weight, so my first thought was clear: *I need to go into prayer and fasting. Lord, is this from You? Is this truly Your will in this season? Is this a distraction?*

Later that night, after my unexpected phone call, I got still before the Lord, and that's when clarity started to settle in my spirit: God wasn't pulling me away from purpose; He was expanding it. This wasn't a detour. It was a divine intersection, and let me just add this: I received that phone call during Holy Week, a time when believers around the world remember the surrender, sacrifice, and resurrection of Jesus Christ. The timing wasn't lost on me. God was resurrecting what I had laid down.

I went to journal about everything that had just happened, and if you don't have a journal, let me encourage you to get one. Write down what you're praying for, what you're believing God for, and when He answers or confirms it. As I opened my journal to write, I flipped back through old entries and came across one from last September, shortly after I completed my third interview with the program. In that entry, I wrote: "Lord, if it's Your will for me to get accepted for the May start date, please confirm it. Either let me see a red cardinal today, or let me receive an email from the school." I have always loved red cardinals. They've been symbolic to me for years. I didn't see one that day, but I got an email. A reply from the school, the very same day I had written that prayer. What made it even more unusual is that I had been waiting nearly two weeks for a response, and they usually reply quickly. That email became the confirmation I asked for, and I had completely forgotten about it until now, but that wasn't the only confirmation.

I started thinking about the dreams I'd had over the years. Dreams where I was already accepted into the CRNA program, heading over to speak with the program director. Dreams where I was rounding on patients as a CRNA. Dreams where someone was asking me questions as a CRNA student. I remembered another journal entry, one I had written the night before one of those dreams. I had asked God once again for confirmation, and that night, I had a dream that I received three pairs of earrings from the university. Each set of earrings was uniquely styled and different in design. I was showing them off to our neighbors, and *you know what's wild?* It's a three-year program.

Each pair of earrings represented a year I would complete in the program. God had been speaking. I just needed to quiet the noise and pay attention. That's how I remember. I write down every dream and prayer. Then I take it before God and ask for clarity. Sometimes, the clarity is immediate. Other times, it's revealed little by little over time, but either way, He always confirms His will. You just have to stay close enough to hear it. This whole experience has been surreal. I surrendered the idol. I gave up the need to control, and God gave it back to me—restored, refined, and wrapped in divine timing.

> ●**Real Talk Moment:**
> God really waited until I stopped gripping the dream out of fear of losing it. When I finally said, "Okay Lord, I trust You", He said, "Perfect. Now watch me work."

Psalm 37:4 (NKJV) says, *"Delight yourself also in the Lord, and He shall give you the desires of your heart."* Don't forget that when you delight in Him, your desires start to align with His will. That's when the promise doesn't feel forced; it flows.

Reflection Question for You

What dream have you been holding onto so tightly that you haven't given God space to breathe on it? Are you willing to lay it down and trust Him to give it back in the way only He can?

Commissioning Prayer

Let me pray over you: *Father, I thank You for Your daughter reading this chapter right now. I thank You that her life is not random and that You have assigned, positioned, and equipped her. I declare that every spirit of fear, anxiety, confusion, and stagnation is broken off her life in the name of Jesus. I speak boldness, clarity, and dominion over her future. God, open her ears to hear You more clearly. Open her eyes to see her assignment. Release fresh fire in her heart to pursue You without fear. May she rise like the Canaanite woman and refuse to let go until she walks in the fullness of what You have called her to do. In Jesus's name, Amen.*

Your Assignment Requires Action

To receive from Jesus requires faith. It is impossible to please God without faith. James 2:17 says, *"So you see, faith by itself isn't enough.*

Unless it produces good deeds, it is dead and useless." True faith isn't proven by what you feel—it's revealed by what you do. The Canaanite woman's faith wasn't quiet. It wasn't convenient. It was persistent, loud, and unrelenting. That's the kind of faith you need to walk in dominion. You need the kind of faith that moves mountains, casts out fear, and changes your life. Setting new goals according to what God is calling you to do can be intimidating, and that requires courage and faith, but you were made for this. You've been assigned, equipped, and anointed to live a life of purpose, authority, and impact. Visit www.eyfbook.com to download the "Faith in Action Blueprint" to help you turn faith into action and walk in the power God has given you.

> **Real Talk Moment:**
> Kingdom impact isn't about having a polished plan. It's about having the guts to walk out what God placed inside of you.

CHAPTER 12
HAVE DOMINION OVER THE EARTH

"You gave them charge of everything you made,
putting all things under their authority."
(Psalm 8:6, NLT)

A Portrait of Dominion: The Proverbs 31 Woman

When you think about a woman who walked in true dominion, not only over her household but over her habits, time, and purpose, the Proverbs 31 Woman is the blueprint. Here's the thing you may not know. The Proverbs 31 Woman wasn't an actual person. She was a poetic description, a vision painted by King Lemuel's mother to show what it looks like when a woman lives with wisdom, discipline, and authority.

She wasn't praised because she was perfect; she was praised because she ruled well. She governed herself well. She woke up early to care for her family, ran a successful business, gave to the poor, and stewarded her time and resources with intention. This description wasn't just about her external works; it was about her posture of the heart. She lived with strength and dignity, not because life was easy, but because she showed up with discipline and faith.

That same capacity is in you. The truth is that the Proverbs 31 Woman would've been the type to manage her home, build her business, mentor others, and still have dinner on the table by 6 PM, with grace and discipline. She would've even had to set boundaries so that her purpose wouldn't be buried under productivity.

Your Calling to Rule Well

"And God said to them, 'Be fruitful and multiply and fill the earth and subdue it and have dominion over the fish of the sea and over the birds of the heavens and over every living thing that moves on the earth." — (Genesis 1:28). For a long time, I believed that if I stayed in my little safe space—family, work routine, and a quiet life—I was doing enough, but God didn't create us to simply survive in a bubble. He called us to lead, influence, and walk in dominion. I was basically playing spiritual hide and seek with my purpose, and trust me, I was hiding way too well.

Why Inconsistency & Busyness Destroy Dominion

I wasn't walking in dominion because I couldn't even govern my own life. I would start off strong in prayer, Bible study, or fitness, and then I'd fall off track. Every time life got busy or discouragement hit me, I'd lose momentum. One day, I heard a pastor say, "Doubt is revealed through inconsistency." That stopped me in my tracks because if I believed in God and if I believed in the calling on my life, why did I keep giving up? It wasn't just inconsistency that destroyed my dominion; it was busyness. It wasn't the good, productive kind of busyness. I'm talking about the kind of busyness that keeps you running in circles without making real progress.

The truth is that not every "good" thing is a God thing. 1 Corinthians 6:12 says, "You say, 'I am allowed to do anything'—but not everything is good for you. And even though 'I am allowed to do anything,' I must not become a slave to anything." Sometimes, the enemy will flood your life with "good" distractions to keep you off track. For example, you may be so busy volunteering, saying "yes" to everyone's needs, attending every event, and pouring out in every ministry. Yet, you've neglected the one assignment God actually called you to focus on in this season. Good things can become distractions if they distract you from your Divine assignment. Busyness without boundaries is a trap. If the enemy can't make you bad, he'll make you busy.

> **💬Real Talk Moment:**
> If the enemy can't steal your salvation, he'll try to steal your schedule. Don't let being busy be the boss of your breakthrough.

Shift Your Mindset: Rule Yourself First

Romans 14:8 says, *"If we live, it's to honor the Lord. And if we die, it's to honor the Lord. So whether we live or die, we belong to the Lord."* Your life belongs to God. You were created to rule, not by controlling others, but by leading yourself under His authority. The Proverbs 31 Woman ruled well because she first ruled herself well. You can't govern your family, career, finances, or calling if you're not governing your mindset, habits, and time.

> **💬Real Talk Moment:**
> If you can't even rule your bedtime, how are you going to rule your business, Woman of God? Start with yourself first.

A Dream of Dominion: Sink or Swim?

One night, I had a dream. I was surrounded by endless water. All around me, people were swimming. Some were gliding confidently. Others were panicking, flailing, and struggling to stay afloat. Tragically, some were face down and lifeless—drowned.

When I woke up, I knew God was showing me a picture of the spiritual condition of many of us. Some of us are confidently swimming, walking in dominion, and fully surrendering to God. Some of us are flailing, overwhelmed by inconsistency, busyness, and distractions. Some are spiritually lifeless—disconnected from God and floating aimlessly. You were never created to drown in life's waters. You were created to rule them. The question is, *will you sink or swim?*

> 🗩**Real Talk Moment:**
> Some of y'all are treading water spiritually, but God's calling you to swim like you've got somewhere to be. Don't settle for survival when you were made for dominion.

Strategies to Cultivate Dominion

Here's how to take control and rule well in every area of your life:

1. Identify Areas Where You Lack Dominion. – Write down the top 3 areas where you feel powerless or inconsistent. (Examples: spiritual life, finances, health, marriage, career.)

2. Pray for God's Wisdom. – Ask God how He wants you to lead in these areas and surrender the areas you've been trying to control without Him.

3. Set Specific, Realistic Goals. – For each area, write ONE tangible goal. Example: "Spend 15 minutes every morning in prayer."

4. Create an Action Plan. – Break your goals down into small, clear steps. Example: To improve finances, make a budget, cut one unnecessary expense, and save the difference.

5. Find Accountability. – Ask a trusted friend, spouse, or mentor to hold you accountable.

6. Reflect God's Character Daily. – Choose one Fruit of the Spirit each week to practice intentionally (love, patience, self-control).

7. Use Your Gifts to Serve. – Identify ways to serve others with your gifts. Examples: Mentoring and teaching others, volunteering, etc.

8. Be a Good Steward of Creation. – Look for small ways to care for what God has entrusted you, whether it's your time, environment, resources, or relationships.

> 🗩**Real Talk Moment:**
> Dominion isn't about being bossy, it's about being Spirit-led, disciplined, and focused on what God is calling you to do.

BOSS Method™ Tie-In: Strategic for Kingdom Impact

A Proverbs 31 Woman didn't wake up and wing it; she had a plan. Walking in dominion requires more than faith; it requires strategy. She reflects the final pillar of the Cultivated BOSS Method™: Strategic for Kingdom Impact. You were never meant to live scattered or reactive. God has called you to live with intention, covered in prayer, and guided by vision. When you strategize with Heaven, you won't just survive, you'll lead with purpose, create with clarity, and walk boldly in the authority God has given you.

Reflection Questions

* *Where in your life have you allowed doubt, busyness, or inconsistency to rule over you?*

* *What specific goals can you set today to begin walking in dominion?*

* *Who can you ask to hold you accountable on this journey?*

* *How can you use your gifts to serve others this week?*

* *What does "dominion" look like for you in this season?*

Spiritual Activation: Commissioning Prayer Over Your Calling

Let me pray over you: *Father God, I lift up every woman who has finished this book. I thank You for her hunger, willingness, and desire to live boldly for You. Lord, remind her that she is not called to play small but to reign with wisdom, love, and authority. Break every cycle of fear, doubt, busyness, and inconsistency in her life. Stir up her gifts. Fill her with clarity and confidence. Let her walk each day like the Proverbs 31 Woman, strong, disciplined, and clothed in dignity. May she swim freely in the waters of life, led by Your Spirit, and never drown in fear again. This is her season to rise and rule. In Jesus's name, Amen.*

Final Charge: Your Cultivated Life Starts Now

I'm walking out what God is calling me to do in this current season. I'm not sure exactly what the future holds, but I know with God on my side, I cannot fail. God can have multiple callings on our lives, but it is up to us to be in a position to receive them, walk in author-ity, and rule over the Earth, living fearlessly and boldly for Him. Romans 12:2 says, *"Don't copy the behavior and customs of this world, but let God transform you into a new person by changing the way you think. Then, you will learn to know God's will for you, which is good and pleasing and perfect."*

Yes, the statement is true—what God has for you is meant for you, but that promise doesn't stand on its own. It only becomes real when you posture yourself in a way for God to pour out what He has for you. You have to do your part to receive it. Your obedience, disci-pline, and surrender are the vessels God will use to release what He's already assigned to your name. Living boldly for God and walking in authority takes time.

> **🗨Real Talk Moment:**
> The promise is real, but the posture is required. God won't pour oil into a cup that's flipped upside down.

At the Cross

Before you walk in dominion and fix your crown and take your place as a cultivated woman of God, you need to revisit the moment that made all of this possible. It doesn't start with confidence or strategy. It starts at the cross, the place of Divine exchange. This was the mo-ment that changed everything.

Imagine this

Jesus walks up to the cross holding everything Heaven has to offer: perfect love, righteousness, peace, authority, purpose, and unshak-able identity. Then you walk up carrying shame. Doubt. Your past. The pressure to be everything for everyone. The labels they put on you. The lies you believed. The guilt you tried to hide. The version of yourself that questioned if you'd ever be enough. He doesn't flinch. He doesn't sigh. He doesn't scold. He just offers all of His to you, and takes all of yours onto Himself. Then He carries your baggage to the cross. That's the kind of love that crowns you in glory.

Jesus didn't just die for sin in a general sense. He died for your anxiety. Your overthinking. Your secret battles with worth. Every silent breakdown behind closed doors. He paid for your ability to rise in authority. He secured your place as a daughter of the King. That's why you can walk in dominion, because He already walked through death to give you life. He didn't just save you, He exchanged Himself for you.

The Divine Exchange: What Jesus Took vs. What He Gave

What He Took	What He Gave
Your shame	His glory
Your fear	His peace
Your sin	His righteousness
Your rejection	His acceptance
Your defeat	His victory

💬Real Talk Moment:

This is just a glimpse of what Jesus gave at the cross. The truth is—He gave everything. For you. For me. For us all. Every exchange was intentional. Every sacrifice was personal, and every gift was sealed in love.

Now you understand. You don't walk in dominion because you're perfect. You walk in dominion because of what happened at the cross. Visit www.eyfbook.com to download the "Cultivated Life Reflection Pack" to seal your journey with reflection, celebration, and the declaration of who you're becoming.

FINAL DECLARATION

I Am a Cultivated BOSS Affirmation

Declare this over yourself: *I am a Cultivated BOSS. I walk boldly in faith because I know the One who called me. I obey God even when the path is unclear, because I trust His voice above all. I am led by the Spirit, not by fear or pressure, and I strategize not for my own success, but for Kingdom impact. My identity is rooted in Christ. My purpose is aligned with Heaven, and my life is a testimony of what happens when a woman fully surrenders to God. I am a Cultivated BOSS, shaped by the Word, empowered by grace, and equipped to walk in divine destiny.*

Sealed for Purpose Prayer

Pray this out loud: *Father, thank You for everything You've revealed to me on this journey. I declare that I won't leave this experience the same. Seal every truth in my heart. Empower me to walk in bold faith, radical obedience, and Spirit-led strategy. Let my life be living proof that surrender births destiny. In Jesus' name, Amen.*

You've been called, cultivated, and commissioned. Now walk it out—Bold in Faith, Obedient to God's Call, Spirit-Led in every step, and Strategic for Kingdom Impact. *You are a Cultivated BOSS. Your "yes" just shifted the atmosphere, and the world will never be the same.*

EPILOGUE

Now that you have reached the end of this book, you have the resources and strategies to propel your relationship with God, enhance clarity in your life, and achieve confidence in who you are through Christ. You have a chance to release everything that God has in store for you, access to His secret wisdom concerning your life, and experience a chance for God to open new doors you never thought possible.

I want to caution you to not just read this book but to actually internalize it. Be open and intentional about your relationship with God. Take heed to these strategies because they will allow you to experience renewal and transformation, leading to a fresh start in your spiritual journey.

In this book, you learned strategies to help you become the kingdom woman God is calling you to be. Here's a brief breakdown:

Chapter 1: Know Your Creator – This chapter helps you understand who God truly is as the source of all life and recognize how spiritual fulfillment is key when seeking satisfaction.

Chapter 2: Understand Your Purpose and Calling – This chapter helps you gain clarity on how to partner with God and actively participate in His plan for your life. Learn how to seek the Gifter instead of the gift.

Chapter 3: Realize that You Are of Royalty – This chapter helps you understand the components of how you were created in God's image, who is Holy, righteous, and perfect in all ways. Learn how to be rooted in your identity through Christ.

Chapter 4: Deliverance and Spiritual Warfare – This chapter helps you renounce negative words and break strongholds over your life to further your spiritual walk with God. Understand the components of how you have the power and authority to do so through the power of the Holy Spirit.

Chapter 5: Master Spiritual Discipline and Maturity – This chapter helps you gain clarity on how to rely on the Holy Spirit to guide you through your spiritual walk. Learn how to give up your will for God's will, set routine actions to grow closer to God, and develop a healthy mindset.

Chapter 6: Walk by the Fruits of the Spirit – This chapter helps you learn about the fruits of the Holy Spirit and understand how to allow God to cleanse and purify your heart. Understand the components of daily repentance and reinforcement necessary to bear good fruit. If you're having a hard time hearing from God, check your fruits!

Chapter 7: Time Management and Eliminating Distractions – This chapter helps you live like those who are wise and make the most of every opportunity. Learn how to uproot distractions, establish priorities with God, and set clear goals with action plans.

Chapter 8: Engage in Prayer and Meditation – This chapter helps you gain clarity on how and what to pray and meditate on. Understand how to recognize your dependence on God and embed the Word of God within yourself.

Chapter 9: Understanding Why and How to Fast. This chapter helps you learn the different types of fasts, discover strategies to fuel your spirit, and understand how to rely on God to equip you with what you need to endure.

Chapter 10: Re-Discover Visions and Values – This chapter helps you write your visions and values down to refocus your life. Learn how to set goals and action plans to execute your visions.

Chapter 11: Set New Goals and Put Faith into Action – This chapter helps you allow God to elevate you by being open and obedient. Gain clarity on how to know when God is calling you into a new season and how to set goals and action plans according to that call.

Chapter 12: Have Dominion Over the Earth – This chapter helps you to know that it's time to walk in authority and rule over the Earth, living fearlessly and boldly for God!

Our days are numbered, and the time has come to start living intentionally for Christ. I want you to move forward and have faith in your own potential. Don't let this book be the end of your journey. It's time to implement these strategies, go deeper with God, and be confident to walk in authority according to who you are called to be. God is beyond ready to partner with you.

REFERENCES

Biblica. (2011). Holy Bible, New International Version (NIV). You-Version. https://www.bible.com

Crossway Bibles. (2016). The Holy Bible, English Standard Version (ESV). YouVersion. https://www.bible.com

Munroe, M. (2021). Discover the hidden you. Destiny Image Publishers, INC.

Public Domain. (n.d.). Holy Bible, King James Version (KJV). You-Version. https://www.bible.com

The Lockman Foundation. (1987). Amplified Bible (AMP). YouVersion. https://www.bible.com

Thomas, E. (n.d.). Discipline is the key [Video]. YouTube. https://www.youtube.com/watch?v=EXtXLqcDM5M

Tyndale House Publishers. (2015). Holy Bible, New Living Translation (NLT). YouVersion. https://www.bible.com

ABOUT THE AUTHOR

Born and raised in Indianapolis, Indiana, Kashana Ruth is a woman of faith, purpose, and passion. Her journey with Christ began in 2001 when she accepted Jesus Christ as her Lord and Savior at Eastern Star Baptist Church. Little did she know then that this decision would become the foundation for the transformative work God would call her to do.

As the Founder and CEO of Women Cultivated in Christ, Kashana is deeply committed to helping career-driven women put God back at the center of their lives. She has worked as a nurse for 12 years, with four of those years as a nurse practitioner. Her professional background is rooted in healthcare, where she dedicated years to serving as a registered nurse and later as a family nurse practitioner. She graduated from Pike High School in Indianapolis before obtaining her Associate Degree in Nursing from Medtech College and her Bachelor's Degree in Nursing from Western Governors University. Most of her nursing career was spent working as an agency medical-surgical nurse, and in her later years, she transitioned into intensive care nursing. Her desire to expand her impact in healthcare led her to complete a Master's Degree as a Family Nurse Practitioner from Olivet Nazarene University, after which she worked as a provider in chronic pain management.

As she sought out her relationship with God, He transitioned her out of her career and led her to write Empower Your Faith. While she excelled in her career, Kashana found herself struggling with having consistency in her prayer life, meditating on God's Word, and truly studying the Bible. Focusing more on professional success than on spiritual growth, she realized the need for a deeper relationship with God. This realization led her to seek Him more intentionally, and *Empower Your Faith* was born through that journey. She wrote this book to help women avoid spiritual stagnation, burnout, and the feeling of being disconnected from God, providing them with a blueprint to prioritize their faith while excelling in their careers.

Kashana is also a mentor and a Christian life coach who recognized the need for a structured path to faith-driven success. Kashana created the Cultivated BOSS Method™ Coaching Program, a four-pillar coaching framework designed to help women become bold in faith and authority, obedient in mind and spirit, Spirit-led and surrendered, and strategic for Kingdom impact. Through this program, she teaches women how to break free from limiting beliefs, cultivate a Kingdom mindset, and align their lives with God's Divine plan.

Her mission is to start a movement of women who are seeking the path God has set for them, walking in obedience, and thriving in faith-driven success. It is her deepest desire to see women flourish spiritually, personally, and professionally because true success means nothing if God isn't in it.

She invites women to join her on this faith, transformation, and Kingdom impact journey. Through her work, she continues to inspire and guide others in cultivating the life God has called them to live.

ADDITIONAL INFORMATION

Continue Your Growth with Women Cultivated in Christ™

Resources and Opportunities Designed to Equip You in Every Season of Your Faith Journey.

COMING SOON: The Cultivated BOSS Method™ Coaching Program

A transformational coaching experience for career-driven Christian women ready to grow in faith, confidence, and spiritual discipline.

Whether you're balancing a busy schedule or searching for clarity in your calling, this coaching experience is designed to help you:

- Realign your life with God.
- Reignite your spiritual discipline.
- Rebuild your confidence from the inside out.
- Learn to lead boldly—in life, work, and faith.

This guided coaching journey is designed to walk with you through faith-based transformation, no matter where you're starting from.

Join the waitlist to get updates about the program length and start dates.

Visit: www.womencultivatedinchrist.com

COMING SOON: THE LEADER'S BUNDLE OFFER

For Women's Groups, Ministries, and Faith-Based Organizations

Bring *Empower Your Faith* to your small group or ministry with our exclusive Leader's Bundle, featuring:

- 10+ Copies of Empower Your Faith
- A complete Group Discussion Guide
- Printable tools: prayers, affirmations, and declarations
- Bonus access to our digital leadership prep toolkit

This is your all-in-one resource for leading women into spiritual growth and alignment.

Join the waitlist to gain access for your group.

Learn more: www.womencultivatedinchrist.com

Because Your Spiritual Growth Doesn't Stop Here, It Multiplies

Stay Equipped. Stay Empowered. Stay Cultivated.

Your journey with God is just getting started. Don't stop here, continue building the habits, confidence, and clarity you need to walk fully in your calling.

Explore free downloads at: www.eyfbook.com

www.ingramcontent.com/pod-product-compliance
Lightning Source LLC
Chambersburg PA
CBHW020418150626
46554CB00014B/1937